Photoshop
Textures
Magic

Photoshop Textures Magic

BY SHERRY LONDON

Photoshop Textures Magic

©1997 Hayden Books

Library of Congress Catalog Number: 96-80333

ISBN: 1-56830-368-8

Copyright © 1997 Hayden Books

Printed in the United States of America 1 2 3 4 5 6 7 8 9 0

Warning and Disclaimer

Trademark Acknowledgments

Publisher Richard Swadley

Associate Publisher John Pierce

Publishing Manager Laurie Petrycki

Managing Editor Lisa Wilson

Marketing Editor Kelli Spencer

The Photoshop Textures Magic Team

Acquisitions Editor
Rachel Byers

Development Editor
Beth Millett

Production Editor
Terrie Deemer

Copy Editor
Jeff Durham

Technical Editor
Kate Binder

Publishing Coordinator
Karen Flowers

Cover Designer
Aren Howell

Book Designer
Gary Adair

Manufacturing Coordinator
Brook Farling

Production Team Supervisors
Laurie Casey
Joe Millay

Production Team
Trina Brown
Dan Caparo
Diana Groth
Laure Robinson
Pamela Woolf

Composed in *Bembo* and *GillSans*

iv

About the Author

Sherry London is a principal of London Computing: PhotoFX, a design and consulting company, and a Contributing Editor for *Computer Artist* magazine. She is the author of *Photoshop 3.0 Special Effects How-To* (Waite Group Press, 1995) and *Photoshop 4.0—An Interactive Course* (Waite Group Press, 1997). She is a contributor to *MacWeek* and *MacUser* magazines, and a sysop on the Adobe Forum on CompuServe. She has lectured at the Thunder Lizard Photoshop Conference and at the Professional Photographers of America conventions. She teaches Photoshop and Pre-press for the Desktop Publishing Certification Program at Moore College of Art and Design in Philadelphia, PA.

Dedication

To my ninth grade art teacher (wherever she may be). She convinced me that I had no art ability, but she also gave me a gift of great value. She taught me how to look at the textures of the natural world and to notice the beauty in the reflection of the sun in a garbage pail.

Acknowledgments

Beth Millett, Rachel Byers, Terrie Deemer, and Kate Binder for making this book the most fun I have ever had on a project. Thanks also to my husband, Norm—as always—for putting up with me for so long and for tolerating a house that is chaotic at best.

Special thanks to Phyllis London for contributing images to the "Bouclé," "Cane," "Stucco," "Thumbprint," and "Wash" techniques; and to Ellen Zucker for contributing images to the "Parched" technique. Thanks to Dave Tiech of Mind of the Machine for the octopus image used in the "Pearls" technique.

v

Hayden Books

The staff of Hayden Books is committed to bringing you the best computer books. What our readers think of Hayden is important to our ability to serve our customers. If you have any comments, no matter how great or how small, we'd appreciate your taking the time to send us a note.

You can reach Hayden Books at the following:

Hayden Books
201 West 103rd Street
Indianapolis, IN 46290
317-581-3833

Email addresses:

America Online:	Hayden Bks
Internet:	hayden@hayden.com

Visit the Hayden Books Web site at
`http://www.mcp.com/hayden/`

Contents

Introduction

I am a fiber artist and fabric designer by training. I cannot remember a time when I did not have some type of needlework or knitting project in hand. Through my love of fiber, I developed a love of pattern and texture.

The basic understanding that you need in order to create these textures is the understanding of how something repeats or generates a "seamless" pattern. I have tried to provide that understanding for you through a variety of seamless tiling techniques listed in the Basics section, and by giving you a large variety of patterns and textures with which to play.

Please enjoy these and try them out. I had a marvelous time writing this book. I hope you take pleasure from working with the techniques as much I relished creating them.

—Sherry

Before You Start

Welcome

Welcome to another volume in the series for creating magic with Photoshop. Like its sisters, *Photoshop Type Magic*, *Photoshop Web Magic*, and *Photoshop Effects Magic*, this book is more than a how-to manual—this book is a what-to guide. The steps in this book tell you exactly what you need to do in order to create exactly what you want. Flip through the thumbtabs to find the texture you want to create and follow the concise, explanatory steps. Or thumb through to discover a texture you never imagined and learn what to do to create it. If you need a little extra help, flip to the Photoshop Basics section. But before you jump in, allow me tell you a little about how this book works. A quick read now will maximize your time later.

System Setup

Here are the system recommendations for creating these effects.

MacOS users: The Adobe Photoshop 4.0 Info box suggests a memory allocation of 21 megabytes (MB) of RAM to run Photoshop. And your system software may need as much as 10MB of RAM. That's a full bowl of soup, but if you've got the memory, then I would recommend setting the Preferred memory size even higher than 21MB. If you don't have 21MB to spare, then just quit all other applications and give it everything you've got.

Windows users: Adobe suggests 32MB of RAM for Photoshop on any 386 or faster processor running Windows 3.1, Windows 95, or Windows NT, but 40MB is better. Quit any application you can before starting Photoshop to maximize the running of the application. Photoshop runs 32-bit native on both Windows 95 and Windows NT operating systems.

It is not crucial, but it will help if you have a CD-ROM drive. A number of the effects in this book use files that are contained on the CD that comes bundled with this book. (See Appendix B, "What's on the CD-ROM," for information on accessing those files.) However, even if you don't have a CD-ROM drive, you still can perform all of the effects described in the book.

Adobe Photoshop 4.0

All of the techniques in this book were created with Adobe Photoshop 4.0, and that's the version I recommend you use. If you're attempting to duplicate these techniques using an earlier version of Photoshop, your results may differ slightly or significantly compared to mine. If you're working with version 3.0, then you still will be able to create all of the textures in the book. However, keep in mind you will need to adjust the instructions for the differences between the two versions. You will see that even some of the old Photoshop features work differently in Photoshop 4.0. Many of the textures in this book use features that were not available in earlier versions of Photoshop.

Conventions

Every image in this book was created initially as an RGB file. You can make your effects in any appropriate color mode, but you should be aware of the variations this will cause as you proceed through the steps. For example, the first new channel created in an RGB file is automatically named Channel #4. But the first new channel created in a CMYK file is named Channel #5. You also should be aware of the differences in the color ranges of the various color modes. Some colors that look great in RGB mode may look like mud after you convert the file's color mode to CMYK. The Lighting Effects filter, for example, will not work in a CMYK or grayscale file.

If you'd like more detailed information about the different color modes, refer to a good general Photoshop book such as *Photoshop 4 Complete*, or to your Photoshop user manuals.

Also, every image was created as a 150-dpi resolution file. (The thumbtab images were created as 300 dpi files.) If you are going to work in a resolution other than 150 dpi, remember that some of the filters and commands will require different settings than the settings I used. Because there are fewer pixels in a 72 dpi image, a Gaussian Blur radius of 5 pixels will blur the image more than if it were a 150 dpi image. Just keep an eye on the figures next to the steps and match the outcome as close as you can.

The Blue Type

As you work through the steps, you will see phrases that are colored a light blue. These phrases are listed in alphabetical order in the Photoshop Basics section. If the phrase in blue asks you to perform a task that you are unfamiliar with, then you can find that phrase in the Photoshop Basics section and follow the instructions on how to perform that task.

Menu Commands

You also will see instructions that look like this:

Filter➝Blur➝Gaussian Blur (2 pixels)

This example asks you to apply the Gaussian Blur filter. To perform this command, click on the Filter menu at the top of the screen and drag down to Blur. When Blur is highlighted a new menu opens to the right, from which you can choose Gaussian Blur.

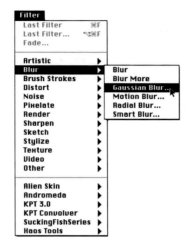

In this example, a dialog box appears asking you for more information. All of the settings that you need to perform each task appear in the text of the step. The previous example tells you to enter 2 pixels as the Radius.

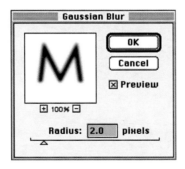

Click OK to blur the image.

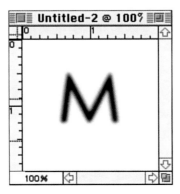

5

Photoshop Textures Magic

Settings

Following each action in the steps, you will find the settings for that feature. These recommended settings are meant to act as guides; the best settings for your effect may vary. As a rule, it is best to match the outcomes that you see in the figures as you progress through the technique. The greatest differences occur when the resolution of your file is significantly different from what I used. The following two images demonstrate the importance of adjusting for resolution differences. A 6-pixel Radius Gaussian Blur was applied to both images.

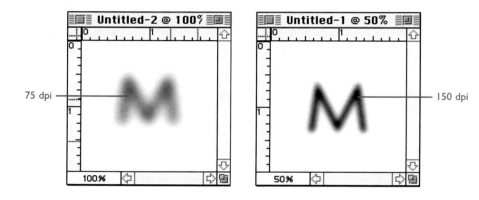

75 dpi

150 dpi

Tips

Throughout the book, you will find additional bits of information that can help you make the most of Photoshop. These tips provide information beyond the basic steps of each lesson.

Photoshop Basics

The goal of this section is to help new and novice users of Photoshop with the simple, basic tasks required to create the effects described and illustrated in this book. Each of the basic tasks described in this section corresponds to the blue highlighted text in the chapters that follow. Here, users can easily find the instructions they need for performing a particular Photoshop task.

This chapter proceeds on two assumptions: that you're creating these textures in Photoshop 4.0; and that you're keeping the Toolbox, and the Brushes, Options, and Layer/Channel/Path palettes open. If one or more of these palettes are closed when you refer to this chapter, you can reopen them by name using the Window menu at the top of the screen. If you're using an earlier version of Photoshop, you can refer to the Photoshop manual for instructions on how to perform these tasks.

Images and Resolution

When you create your own textures, you need to know where you are going to use them. If you are planning to use the texture in a multimedia presentation or on the Web, you only need to work at 72 ppi—this is screen resolution. What you see onscreen is what you are going to see when you display the final texture. If you are going to print the texture, you are in a different ball game. Printing typically needs a 300 ppi resolution. If you have a 50-pixel square file, the image that would be larger than one-half inch onscreen will now be only one-sixth of an inch. Fine detail—especially from the Add Noise filter—will be lost.

Although I generally think it is a bad idea to greatly enlarge your images, it will not hurt many of the textures—especially the "noisy" ones. If you want to preserve as much of the noise as you can, use the Nearest Neighbor interpolation when you scale up the image. This keeps your file from anti-aliasing as it is enlarged. It will look pixellated onscreen, but should print so that it looks like the texture before you enlarged it (assuming that you do not enlarge a texture more than 300%).

The Toolbox

If you're not familiar with Photoshop's Toolbox, there's no reason to panic. With a bit of experimentation, it doesn't take long to learn each tool's individual functions. This representation of the Toolbox will help both beginners and experts find the tools they need.

Photoshop Textures Magic

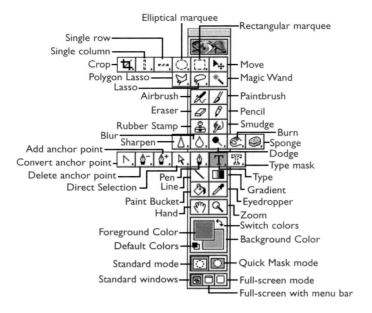

Basic Photoshop Tasks

Add a Horizontal or Vertical Guide

Turn on the Rulers (Command-R)[Control-R]. Place your cursor on the horizontal or vertical ruler. Press the mouse button, and drag a guide into the image.

Choose a Foreground or Background Color

Shortcut: Press D to change colors to their defaults: black for the foreground, and white for the background. (Note: If you are working on a layer mask or in a channel, pressing D will give you white foreground and black background.)

Press X to switch the foreground color with the background color.

To change the foreground or background color, click on either the Foreground icon or the Background icon.

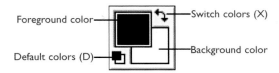

Foreground color —
Default colors (D) —
Switch colors (X)
Background color

The Color Picker dialog box appears, which enables you to choose a new foreground or background color by moving and clicking the cursor (now a circle) along the spectrum box, or by changing specific RGB, CMYK, or other percentage values. Note that the Foreground and Background icons on the Toolbox now reflect your color choices.

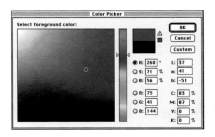
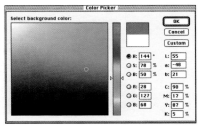

Change the Blending Mode

In many techniques you will be instructed to change from Normal to another blending mode. This may refer to the Options palette for some tools, or the Layers palette, or the Fade dialog box. Blending mode influences how the pixels from two sources will combine.

To change from Normal mode to any of 16 alternatives, first click the pop-up menu, and then drag to your choice of mode. Consult your Photoshop User Guide for details on how each blending mode works.

9

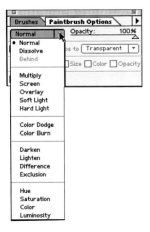

Convert to a New Mode

To convert from one color mode to another, click on the Image menu at the top of the screen and scroll down to the Mode command. You then can scroll down to select the mode of your preference. If you want to switch from CMYK mode to multichannel mode, for example, you choose Image➧Mode➧Multichannel. The check mark to the left of CMYK will move down to Multichannel, indicating that you are now in multichannel mode.

TIP Remember that there is a different range of colors available for each color mode. No matter what color mode the file is in onscreen, for example, your printer (if it prints in color) is going to print your work in CMYK. Because the color ranges for RGB and CMYK are different, you should convert your RGB image to CMYK before printing. Otherwise, you may be in for a big surprise when your bright green prints as a dull tan.

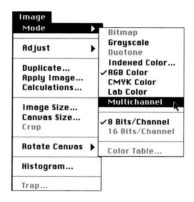

Create a Layer Mask

To create a layer mask, click the Layer Mask icon at the bottom of the Layers palette. A layer mask is used to mask out (or hide) parts of a layer. Painting with black hides an area, and painting with white reveals it. Dragging a layer mask to the trash icon at the bottom of the Layers palette enables you to make its effects permanent or delete it. Here the layer mask is active, indicated by the black border around it and the mask icon in the active layer.

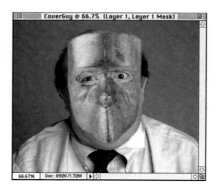

Create an Adjustment Layer

Shortcut: Press the (Command)[Control] key and click on the New Layer icon at the bottom right of the Layers palette.

Select Layer palette menu➡New Adjustment Layer.

The resulting dialog box enables you to select the type of adjustment layer—Levels and Hue/Saturation are the ones most often used here. You can also change the blending mode of the adjustment layer at the same time.

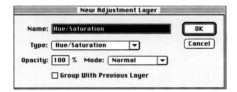

Create a New Background Layer

This works in an image only if it does not contain a Background layer. Press the (Option)[Alt] key and click on the New Layer icon. This opens up a dialog box. In the blending mode list, scroll down to the very last entry in the menu. It will say "Background." Select this as the mode and it creates a new Background layer.

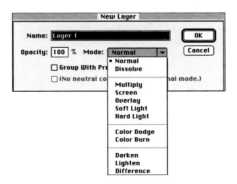

Photoshop Textures Magic

Create a New Channel

Shortcut: Click the New Channel icon on the Channels palette.

To create a new channel, choose New Channel from the Channels palette pop-up menu. You will not see the Options dialog box if you use the shortcut.

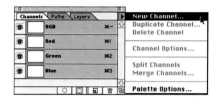

Use the Channel Options dialog box to establish your settings. Unless noted otherwise, we used the default settings when creating a new channel. This figure shows Photoshop's default settings.

Create a New File

Shortcut: Press (Command-N)[Control-N].

To create a new file, choose File➡New. The New dialog box appears, which is where you name your new file and establish other settings. See the "Before You Start" section for information on the conventions that were used when creating new files for the type effects in this book.

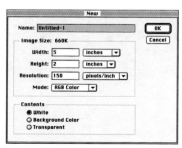

Create a New Layer

Shortcut: Click the New Layer icon on the Layers palette. You will not see the Options dialog box if you use the shortcut unless you press the (Option)[Alt] key as you click on the New Layer icon.

To create a new layer, choose New Layer from the Layer palette pop-up menu, or choose Layer➡New➡Layer.

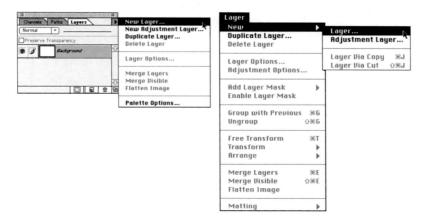

The New Layer dialog box opens, which is where you name the new layer and establish other settings.

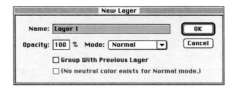

Create Layer 0

Double-click the Background layer of an image. In the dialog box, press (Return)[Enter] and the layer is automatically named Layer 0. This action "detaches" the layer from the background (you no longer have a Background layer) and allows the layer to contain transparency (though it does not add any transparency to an image that is already in the layer).

Define a Clone Source

Select the Rubber Stamp tool. Place the cursor at the location from which you wish to start copying. Press the (Option)[Alt] key and click the mouse. This defines the start of the cloning operation. Move the cursor to another location and press the mouse to paint.

13

Photoshop Textures Magic

Define a Pattern

Select➡All (or create a selection using the rectangular Marquee tool). Select Edit➡Define Pattern. Now you can fill with this pattern.

Delete a Channel

To delete a channel, go to the Channels palette and select the channel you want to delete; drag it to the Trash icon at the lower-right corner (just like dragging an icon to the Recycling Bin in Windows 95 or to the Trash in the MacOS Finder). You also can select the channel you want to delete, and choose Delete Channel from the Channels palette menu.

 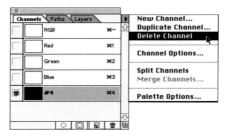

Delete a Layer

To delete a layer, go to the Layers palette and select the layer you want to delete; drag it to the Trash icon at the lower-right corner (just like dragging an icon to the Recycling Bin in Windows 95 or to the Trash in the Mac OS Finder). You also can select the layer you want to delete, and choose Delete Layer from the Layers palette menu or from the Layers menu.

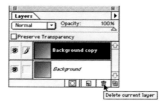 

Deselect a Selection

Shortcut: Press (Command-D)[Control-D].

To deselect a selection, choose Select➡None. The marquee disappears.

Drag and Drop

This technique *is* a shortcut. It eliminates copying to and pasting from the clipboard. With two images open, select an area from the source image and drag it over to the destination image, using the Move tool. A new layer is created automatically.

Shortcut: Press (Command)[Control] to access the Move tool.

Drag and Drop Centered

Before you drag the selection from one image to another, press the Shift key and keep it pressed until the selection is in its new home. This works whether you drag the selection from the image itself or you drag the layer from the Layers palette. For this to consistently work correctly, the two images must be the same size.

Drag the Marquee

There are many places in the book where you are asked to create a rectangular marquee of a fixed size. The instruction, drag the marquee, requires you to place your cursor in the image, press the mouse button, and move the marquee to the instructed place in the image *without* letting go of the mouse button. If you learn to place and drag the marquee in one movement, you can easily get the fixed size marquee into any corner of the image without fear of dragging off of the image. If you create the marquee in this manner, it cannot be dragged outside of the image boundaries. Should you let go of the mouse button before the marquee is in its desired location, you will not be able to position it accurately. If this happens, deselect and try it again.

Duplicate a Channel or Layer

Shortcut: Click the channel or layer you want to duplicate, and drag it on top of the New Channel or New Layer icon. This keeps the layer or channel within the *same* document as the original. Unless the menu command below is explicitly stated, you should use the shortcut.

To create a duplicate of a channel or layer, make it active and then select Duplicate Channel or Duplicate Layer from the appropriate palette menu. This enables you to duplicate the layer or channel and place it, if you want, into another existing image or

15

into a new image of its own. You will always see explicit instructions (written Layer➡ Duplicate Layer or Channels palette menu➡Duplicate Channel) when you are asked to create a duplicate layer or channel in this manner. The reason to use this method is to copy the layer or channel into a new document.

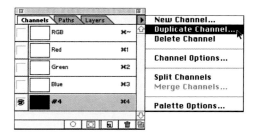

A new copy of the channel you selected for duplication is created automatically, and the Duplicate Channel dialog box appears.

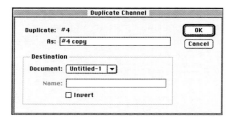

Duplicate the Image

Select Image➡Duplicate. You usually are not asked to name the new image, though you certainly may if you want. Sometimes, you will be told to select Image➡Duplicate (Merged layers only). Click the checkbox in the dialog box. This flattens the layers in the image as it copies it.

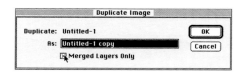

Enter/Exit Quick Mask

Shortcut: Press Q to enter and exit the Quick Mask mode.

Click the Quick Mask icon to switch to Quick Mask mode; conversely, click the Standard mode icon to return to Standard mode.

16

Essentially, a Quick Mask is a temporary channel. When you're in Quick Mask mode, you can use any of the Photoshop tools and functions to change the selection without changing the image. When you switch back to Standard mode, you'll have a new selection.

Enter the Text

Before entering the text using the standard Type tool, make sure that the foreground color is set to your desired text color. If you are entering text into a layer, the standard Type tool will create a new layer for the type.

To enter the text, select the Type tool, and then click anywhere in the image to open the Type Tool dialog box. Type the text in the large box at the bottom of the dialog box, and make your attribute choices from the options. Unless noted otherwise in the instructions, always make sure that you have the Anti-Aliased box checked.

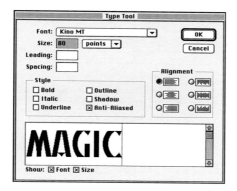

After clicking OK, move the type into position with the Move tool.

Fade the Effect

Shortcut: (Shift-Command-F)[Shift-Control-F] opens a dialog box for fading the last filter or Image➡Adjust command used and changing its blending mode.

To fade the last filter applied, or some other effects such as Invert, choose Filter➡Fade. The Fade slider acts like a partial undo for the last effect you applied. The Blending Mode pop-up menu enables you to determine how the pixels of the before and after versions of the image are combined.

Fill a Selection with Foreground or Background Color

First, choose a foreground or background color you want to use (see page 8 in this section for instructions). Keep the selection active and press (Option-Delete) [Alt-Backspace] to fill the selection with the foreground color. If you are in the Background layer, then you can press (Delete)[Backspace] to fill the selection with the background color. To fill a transparent area with the background color, first turn off Preserve Transparency for that layer, then press (Command-Delete)[Control-Backspace].

You also can fill in your selections by choosing Edit➥Fill, or press (Shift-Delete) [Shift-Backspace] to open the Fill dialog box.

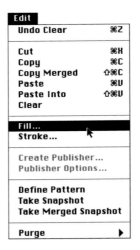

This causes the Fill dialog box to appear, enabling you to establish the Contents option, the Opacity, and the Blending Mode you want to use.

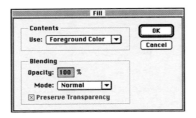

TIP If a selection is empty (a transparent area of a layer) and the Preserve Transparency option is turned on for that layer, then you will not be able to fill the selection. To fill the selection, simply turn off the Preserve Transparency option before filling it.

TIP If you want to fill only the areas of a layer that contain non-transparent pixels, you can either turn on Preserve Transparency, or press the Shift key along with the other keystrokes (depending upon whether you are trying to fill with foreground or background color).

Fill a Selection with Pattern

With a pattern defined, press (Shift-Delete)[Shift-Backspace]. You also can fill your selections by choosing Edit➤Fill.

This causes the Fill dialog box to appear, allowing you to change the Contents option to Pattern, and set the Opacity and the blending mode.

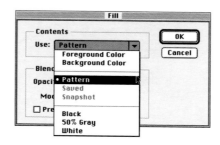

Flatten an Image

To flatten an image (merge all the layers into a single layer), choose Flatten Image from the Layers palette menu, or choose Layer➤Flatten Image.

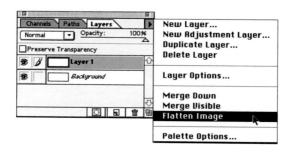

19

Load Brushes

To load another library of brushes, choose Load Brushes in the Brush palette pop-up menu. You can choose whether to "append" additional brushes to the default library or replace the defaults. I recommend you append the Assorted Brushes that come with Photoshop. I've also included a few custom brushes in the Presets folder on the CD-ROM that comes with this book.

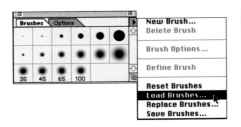
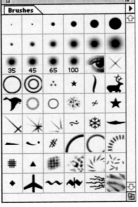

Load a Selection

Shortcut: Hold down the (Command)[Control] key and click the channel (on the Channels palette) that contains the selection you want to load.

To load a selection, choose Select➡Load Selection. This brings up the Load Selection dialog box, in which you can establish document, channel, and operation variables.

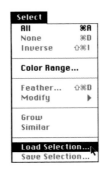
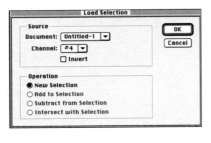

Make a Channel Active

To make a channel active for editing or modification, click on its thumbnail or name on the Channels palette.

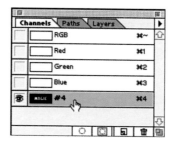

You can tell the channel is active if it is highlighted with a color.

Make a Layer Active

To make a layer active, click on its thumbnail or name in the Layers palette.

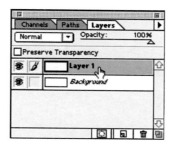

You can tell the layer is active if it is highlighted with a color.

Make a Layer Visible/Invisible

To make a layer visible or invisible, click in the left-most column in the Layers palette. If an eye appears, then the layer is visible. If the column is empty, then that layer is hidden (invisible).

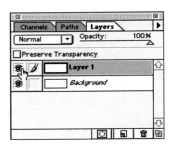 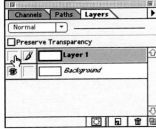

Make an Image Seamless

Center Cross Method: Select the Lasso tool. Select Filter➡Other➡Offset (Wrap Around). Make the Horizontal and Vertical distances one-half of the image dimensions. Draw a selection in the shape of a fat cross around the area where the Offset filter joined the original corners of the image. Choose Select➡Feather, and pick a large feather. Reapply the Offset filter to the selection.

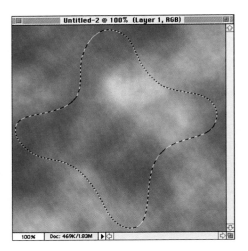

Masked Offset Method: Use the finished tile. Duplicate the Background layer. Select Filter➡Other➡Offset (Wrap Around). Set the Horizontal and Vertical distances to one-half of the image dimensions. Create a layer mask. Use black, the Paintbrush tool, and a large, soft brush. Brush out the center seam line by painting over the area on the layer mask.

Create a new layer. (Option)[Alt] Merge Visible to a new layer. Select Filter➡Other➡ Offset (Wrap Around). Create a layer mask. Use black, the Paintbrush tool, and the soft brush. Brush out the seam line near the edges by painting over the area on the layer mask.

Create a new layer. (Option)[Alt] Merge Visible to a new layer. Select Filter➡Other➡ Offset (Wrap Around). Check to make sure that your image is seamless. It should be. Touch-up using the layer mask if it is not.

Mosaic Method: Double-click the rectangular Marquee and set the fixed size to the current size of your tile. If the tile is in the Background layer, double-click the Background layer in the Layers palette to "raise" the layer to Layer 0. Press (Enter) [Return] in the dialog box—the layer is automatically named Layer 0. Select Image➡ Canvas Size and double the image dimensions either numerically or by selecting 200% for each dimension. Place the anchor in the top-left square. Click OK. Drag the Marquee to the top-left square and copy it to the clipboard (Command-C)[Control-C]. Drag the Marquee into the top-right corner of the image. Edit➡Paste. You will get a new layer. Select Layer➡Transform➡Flip Horizontal. Drag the Marquee into the bottom-left corner. Edit➡Paste. Select Layer➡Transform➡Flip Vertical. Drag the Marquee into the bottom-right corner. Edit➡Paste. Select Layer➡Transform➡Flip Vertical. Select Layer➡Transform➡Flip Horizontal. You have a perfectly seamless tile.

23

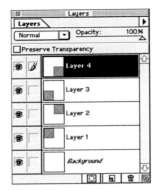

Rubber Stamp Method: After you have offset the image, define a clone source that is not on a seam line. Use the Rubber Stamp tool to cover over the seam line with bits and pieces of other parts of the pattern.

Name/Rename a Layer

To change the name of a layer, double-click its name in the Layers palette and type the new name in the Layer Options dialog box.

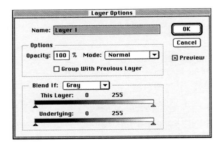

(Option)[Alt] Merge Visible

Shortcut: Press (Shift-Command-Option-E)[Shift-Control-Alt-E].

This command creates a combined picture of all of the visible layers in your image and places it in the active layer. You are usually asked to create a new layer before this command is given, as you must have an empty layer for this to work properly. Press the (Option)[Alt] key and select Layer➡Merge Visible from either the Layers menu or the Layers palette menu. The advantage to this command is that it enables you to keep all of the layers but still have one combined layer that can be manipulated as a single entity. This is one of the most useful and least documented features in Photoshop.

Place an Image

Use File➡Place to bring an EPS (Encapsulated PostScript) image into an open Photoshop document. The image will appear in a bounding box that can be manipulated before anchoring with a click of the (Return)[Enter] key. A new layer is created automatically with the name of the EPS file.

Position a Layer

To move a layer's position in the Layers palette list, click on the layer you want to move in the Layers palette and drag it up or down the list of layers to the place you want to move it. As you drag the layer, the lines between the layers will darken to indicate where the layer will fall if you let go.

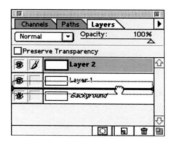

Reduce a Layer's Opacity

Drag the Opacity slider in the Layers palette toward the left. If you need to increase the opacity, drag it toward the right.

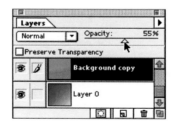

Return to the Composite Channel

Shortcut: Press (Command-~)[Control-~].

If you want to return to the composite channel, click on its thumbnail or title (RGB, CMYK, Lab). The composite channel always will be the first one in the list.

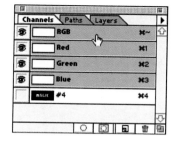

If you are in an RGB file, then Channels 0 through 3 should now be active because each of the R, G, and B channels are individual parts of the RGB image.

Save a File

To save a file, choose File➡Save As. This displays the Save As dialog box, in which you name your new file and choose a format in which to save it.

File format selection depends on what you have in your file, what you want to keep when you save it, and what you're going to do with the file after it is saved. Consult a detailed Photoshop book, such as *Photoshop 4 Complete*, for more guidance on which file format is best for your needs.

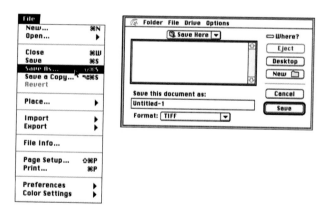

Save a Selection

Shortcut: Click the Save Selection icon on the Channels palette.

To save a selection, choose Select➡Save Selection.

26

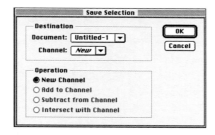

The Save Selection dialog box opens. Choose your options and click OK to save the selection.

Scale Up

Select Image➡Image Size. Check the Resample Image box at the bottom of the Image Size dialog box. Increase the number of pixels in the image. This instruction will usually tell you to change the Interpolation Method to Nearest Neighbor as well.

Switch Foreground/Background Colors

Shortcut: Press X to switch the foreground and background colors.

To switch the foreground and background colors, click on the Switch Colors icon. This flips the two colors shown in this icon only, and does not affect the rest of the image.

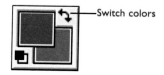

Switch to Default Colors

Shortcut: Press D to switch to the default foreground and background colors.

To change the foreground and background colors to black and white respectively, click on the Default Colors icon.

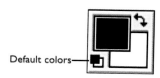

Turn On/Off Preserve Transparency

To turn on or off the Preserve Transparency option for a particular layer, first make that layer the active layer. Then, click the Preserve Transparency checkbox on the Layers palette. This option is not available for the Background layer.

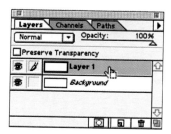

Vary Pressure

If you are using a graphics tablet and pressure-sensitive stylus you can vary the brush size, color, or opacity as you paint by varying your pen pressure; check the appropriate boxes in the Options palette for a tool to vary any or all of these three characteristics.

If you are using a mouse, you can specify a number of steps in the Fade field to make a stroke that feathers out. The higher the number of steps, the slower the fade.

Changing the value on the Opacity slider is effective for both mouse and tablet users.

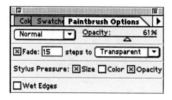

A bouclé is fabric woven from thick, fuzzy, textured yarns. This effect creates a heavy texture that makes wonderful fabric. I'd love to have this fabric in a winter coat! You can make this texture seamless with a bit of extra work.

1 Create a new file. I used one at 400×400 pixels. Choose Filter➡ Texture➡Grain (Intensity: 100, Contrast: 50, Grain Type: Clumped).

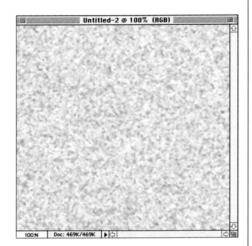

2 Select Filter➡Brush Strokes➡Ink Outlines (Stroke Length: 4, Dark Intensity: 20, Light Intensity: 10).

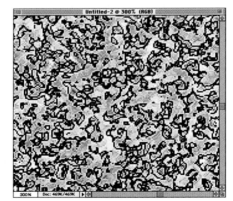

3 Create a new layer (Layer 1) by holding down the (Option)[Alt] key and clicking on the New Layer icon. In the dialog box, change the blending mode to Multiply and check the box marked Fill with Multiply— neutral color (white). Choose Filter➡Texture➡Texturizer (Texture: Burlap, Scaling: 200, Relief: 4, Light Direction: Top).

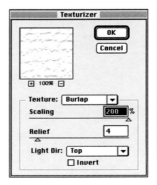

4 The filter does not show up. Choose Image➡Adjust➡Levels (Command-L)[Control-L]. Drag the black Input slider until it is under the place where the black pixels on the graph start to increase. I chose 220 for my image.

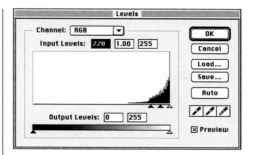

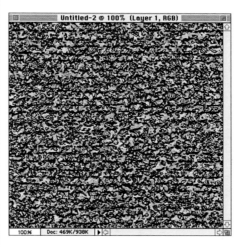

5 Create a new layer (Layer 2). Merge the visible layers to this blank layer (Shift-Command-Option-E)[Shift-Alt-Control-E]. This is a way to have your cake and eat it too. You can add a filter to the combined layer, but you don't lose your originals. Select Filter➡Brush Strokes➡Angled Strokes (Direction Balance: 50, Stroke Length: 50, Sharpness: 3).

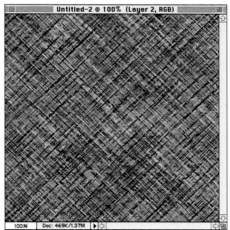

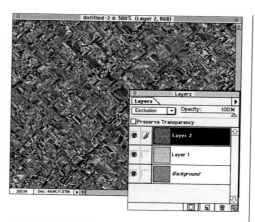

6 Change the blending mode to Exclusion.

VARIATIONS

If you want to make the image into a seamless pattern, select Filter➡ Other➡Offset (Wrap Around) and set the distances to half of your image size. For my 400×400 pixel image, I offset 200 pixels to the right and 200 pixels down. Make the pattern seamless using the Rubber Stamp method. In most cases, you will have little or nothing to touch up. Select➡All. Define the pattern. Create a new file at the desired size. Fill with pattern.

To make a darker texture with bright highlights, use Difference mode in Step 6 instead of Exclusion mode.

To get a texture that is fuzzy, but does not look woven, stop after Step 4 and change the blending mode to Exclusion.

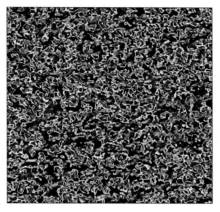

Try making a fabric with darker flecks of yarn. In Step 3, choose Filter➥Pixelate➥Crystalize with a Cell size of 10. Omit Step 4. ■

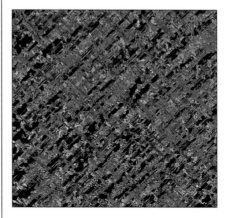

Bricks

Act color
swatches

Bricks are another deceptively simple texture. You can draw an accurate rendition of a brick—which is simply a rectangle—and repeat it quite quickly, but it will probably not look real. Bricks that are too perfect practically scream "computer-generated." Here's how to make bricks that could almost fool the wolf.

1 Create a new file. Mine is 300×300 pixels. This is the template in which you will create the outlines of the bricks. Luckily for you, you really only have to build it once—as long as you don't create your bricks inside of it, you can re-use it for any size project. Turn on the Rulers (Command-R)[Control-R]. Create a new channel. Invert the channel (Command-I)[Control-I] so that it is white. Add vertical guides at the 0, 75, 150, 225, and 300 pixels marks on the top ruler. Add a horizontal guide every 50 pixels on the side ruler (including the 0 and the 300 pixel position). The guides divide the file into 24 pieces.

2 Resize the window so that it is a little bit larger than the image. Double-click the Line tool. Set the Line width to the relative thickness that you want between the bricks. I used a Line width of 6 pixels. Switch the foreground color to black. Channel #4 is active. Select View➡Snap to Guides. Cover all of the horizontal guides with the Line tool (press the Shift key to keep the line straight). You get a more reliable line if you start dragging the cursor from outside of the image on the guide and release the mouse button only after you are clear of the image on the other side. If you don't do this, you risk leaving some needed pixels white.

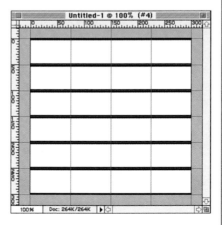

3 Double-click the rectangular Marquee tool. Make certain that Feather is set to 0. Set a fixed size to 300 pixels wide × 50 pixels high. Drag the Marquee to select the top 1/6 of the image. Because Snap to Guides is on, the Marquee will snap to the exact locations needed after you drag it into the vicinity. Hold down the Shift key and drag the Marquee to select the third and fifth sections of the image as well.

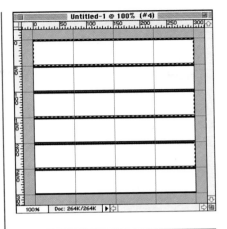

4 Cover *every other* vertical guide with the Line tool. You create three lines (over the first, third, and fifth guide lines).

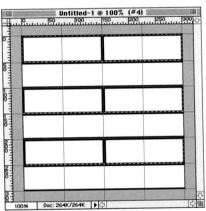

5 Reverse the selection (Select➡ Inverse). Draw straight lines over the remaining two uncolored guide lines. Deselect. Turn off the guides (Command-;)[Control-;].

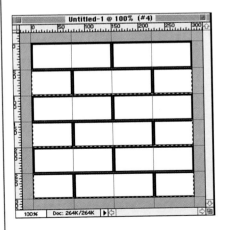

35

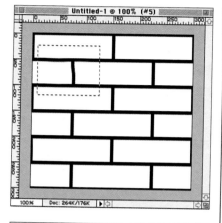

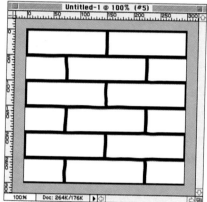

6 You now have a perfect grid block for creating bricks. Nature is not perfect, however, so if you want to add some realism, you need to distress the outline. Duplicate Channel #4 (Channel #5). This allows you to keep one unadulterated copy for future needs. Double-click the rectangular Marquee tool. Change the Style to Normal. Select an area in Channel #5 that is centered on a vertical line. Apply Filter→Distort→ Twirl. Keep the setting somewhere between + or − 16. You want to subtly move the line off of the perpendicular. The key word here, though, is *subtly*. Use too high a setting and your bricks will look decidedly odd. Continue to make selections and apply the Twirl filter with a variety of low settings. You can press (Command-Option-F) [Control-Alt-F] to reapply the same filter with new settings.

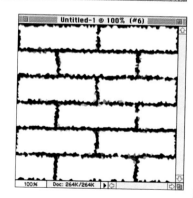

7 Duplicate Channel #5 (Channel #6). This way, you can play with additional changes to the mortaring for the bricks and not have to re-do the Twirl filter. Select Filter→ Pixelate→Crystallize. Select a cell size smaller than 11. I used a cell size of 6.

8 Reapply the Crystallize filter (Command-Option-F)[Control-Alt-F] and change the cell size to something smaller. I used a cell size of 3. The outlines of the bricks are nicely irregular.

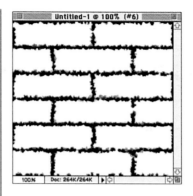

9 Select Filter➡Blur➡Gaussian Blur. I used a Radius of 2.0. Keep the setting between about 1.0 and 3.0.

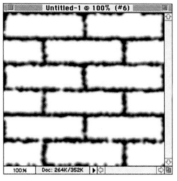

10 This step is optional. Look at the blurred lines. If you see areas where the line is very thin or not there, that means that you will have no mortaring on your bricks in that location. Although the mortar can get thin, it should always be present. Also, areas that are too dissimilar cause the viewer's eye to notice the repeat—which is something that you really want to avoid. Now—with that buildup…with Channel #6 active, load the selection in Channel #4. Reverse the selection (Select➡Inverse). Choose Select➡Modify➡Contract. I contracted the selection by 2 pixels. Fill with black. The only purpose of this step is to make sure that there is some part of a mortar line all along the bricks. Deselect.

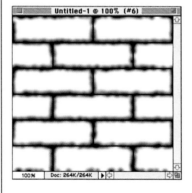

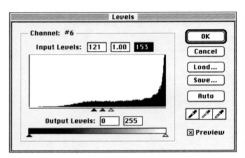

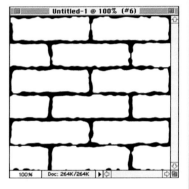

11 Select Image➡Adjust➡Levels. Drag the right and left Input sliders until they are quite close to each other. This sharpens the blur that you applied by forcing many of the gray levels to white or black. You can control the thickness of the line by the location of the three sliders. The closer that three sliders are to the right, the thicker the line will be. If all three sliders are toward the left, the mortar will be very thin. I kept the sliders a bit to the left of center. Save the template file.

12 It's time to build the brick surface. Create a new file the same size as the template file (300×300). Change the foreground color to a brick color. I used RGB: 100, 36, 30. You can also load the Brick.Act color swatches from the *Photoshop Textures Magic* CD-ROM. This palette is taken from a photograph of real bricks and includes a variety of brick colors. Fill the new image with foreground color.

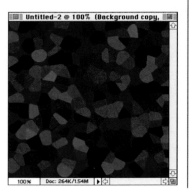

13 You need to add a variety of colors to this tile to simulate the range of colors in real brick. There are many ways to do this. For now, switch foreground/background colors and then select Filter➡ Pixellate➡Pointillize. I used a cell size of 30. Any number from 12 to 40 is fine.

14 Choose Filter➡Blur➡Motion Blur (Angle: 81°, Distance 118). The Angle is just a little bit off of 90°. The Distance is long enough to get a run of color without wiping out the color differences. Select Filter➡Blur➡Gaussian Blur. I used a Radius of 6.8. The larger the cell size that you used in Step 13, the larger of a blur Radius you will need to use here. The idea is to create a range of colors that blend softly.

15 Now you are ready to create surface texture on the brick. The surface texture is a mix of two Hard Light maps. Create a new layer. Switch to default colors. Choose Filter➡Render➡Clouds. Select Image➡Adjust➡Posterize and choose 5 levels.

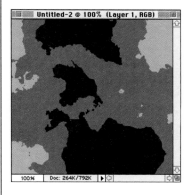

16 Change the background color to RGB: 128, 128, 128 (neutral medium gray).

17 Apply these filters *exactly*. Choose Filter➡Stylize➡Emboss (Angle: 136°, Height: 4 pixels, Amount: 100). Select Filter➡Stylize➡Find Edges. Select Filter➡Blur➡Gaussian Blur (0.6). Choose Filter➡Pixelate➡Pointillize (3). Select Image➡Adjust➡Desaturate. Select Filter➡Noise➡Add Noise (Amount: 42, Distribution: Gaussian, Monochromatic). Select Filter➡Blur➡Gaussian Blur (0.6) Choose Filter➡Stylize➡Emboss (Angle: 136°, Height: 2 pixels, Amount: 100). Select Filter➡Blur➡Gaussian Blur (0.3). This series of filters produces the pitted surface texture on the bricks.

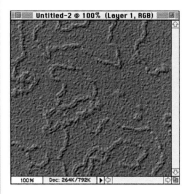

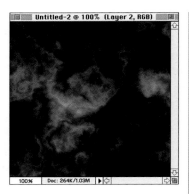

18 Change the blending mode to Hard Light. Switch to default colors. Create a new layer. Choose Filter➡Render➡Clouds. Select Filter➡Render➡Difference Clouds. Apply the Difference Clouds filter approximately 20 times. This increases the internal complexity of the cloud structure.

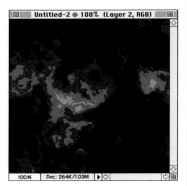

19 Select Image➡Adjust➡ Posterize. (7 levels). This is a much more complex structure than the one produced in Step 15.

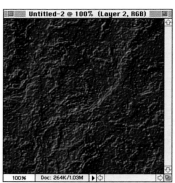

20 Choose Filter➡Stylize➡Emboss (Angle: 136°, Height: 3 pixels, Amount: 100). Change the blending mode to Hard Light.

21 Your image will probably have a bit more shine than brick usually contains. Make Layer 2 active (if it is not already). Select Image➡ Adjust➡Curves. Use the Pencil in the Curves dialog to match the setting shown. Your surface texture is complete.

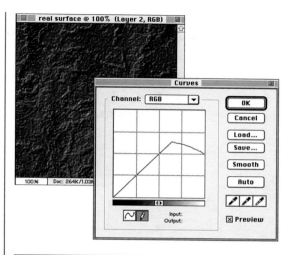

22 Finally—it is time to create the bricks. Make the saved Brick Template document active. Select Image➡Duplicate➡OK. Work in the duplicate. Choose Image➡ Apply Image. Select the brick surface image as the Source (mine is called Untitled-2). Use the Merged layers, RGB channel as shown.

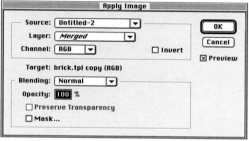

23 Switch the foreground color to a good mortar color. I chose RGB: 182, 162, 148, which is a warm blush gray. Create a new layer. Load the selection in Channel #6 (Command-Option-6)[Control-Alt-6]. Invert the selection (Select➡ Inverse). Fill with foreground color.

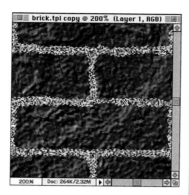

24 Select Filter➡Noise➡Add Noise (Distribution: Gaussian, Monochromatic). I used an Amount of 76.

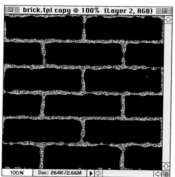

25 Create a new layer. Invert the selection (Select➡Inverse). Switch to default colors. Fill with foreground color. Deselect. This creates the basis for raising the bricks away from the mortar.

26 Choose Filter➡Stylize➡Emboss (Angle: 136°, Height: 5 pixels, Amount: 100). Select Filter➡Blur➡Gaussian Blur (2.0). You see gray bricks with a slight highlight and shadow. Change the blending mode to Hard Light. Now the gray disappears and only the highlight and shadow are left.

27 The bricks are fairly close to being finished, but the brick is so realistic that it seems a pity not to make the mortar a little more natural as well. Create a new layer. Load the selection in Channel #6 (Command-Option-6)[Control-Alt-6]. Invert the selection (Select➡ Inverse). Select Filter➡Render➡ Clouds. Select Filter➡Noise➡Add Noise (Distribution: Gaussian, Monochromatic). I used an Amount of 76. The Clouds filter gives a random shading to the mortar and the noise adopts that shading. Reduce the layer opacity to about 60%.

28 The mortar from Step 27 needs to gain some color. Duplicate Layer 1 (the original mortar) and position the layer at the top of the Layers list. Change the blending mode to Color.

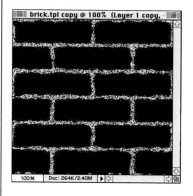

29 If you want a final touch of realism—for use in an onscreen presentation or on the Web (this will not survive the printing process as effectively), in the Channels palette, duplicate Channel #6 (Channel #7). Invert the channel (Command I) [Control-I]. Load the selection in Channel #7. Choose Select➡ Modify➡Expand (3 pixels). Choose Select➡Feather (3 pixels). Select Filter➡Noise➡Add Noise (Distribution: Gaussian, Monochromatic). I used an Amount of 200.

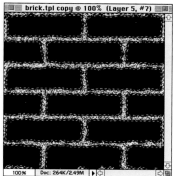

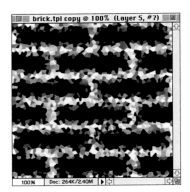

30 Deselect. Choose Filter➡ Pixelate➡Crystallize. I used a cell size of 9. You need a fairly small cell size to leave values of gray "outside the lines"—as if a messy bricklayer splattered mortar around a bit. Choose Image➡Adjust➡Equalize.

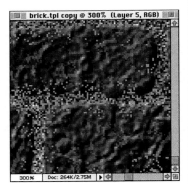

31 Return to the composite channel. Create a new layer. Load the selection in Channel #7. Double-click the Airbrush tool and change the mode for the Airbrush to Dissolve. Set the Pressure to about 6%. Switch the foreground color to the mortar color that you used. Hide the marching ants (Command-H)[Control-H]. Quickly brush over the image leaving bits of mortar outside the mortar lines. The image shows a close-up of noise on the bricks.

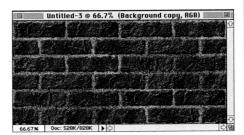

32 You can now build the final pattern tile. Select Image➡Duplicate ➡Merged Layers only. Duplicate the Background layer. Select Image➡Canvas Size. Double the width of the image (600 pixels) and anchor the image in the top-left. Select Filter➡Other➡Offset (Horizontal: 300, Vertical: 200, Wrap Around). This setting keeps the pattern accurate as you offset. By offsetting the image, you more thoroughly randomize the bricks and make it harder to see the repeat.

33 Select➡All. Define the pattern. Create a new file of the desired dimensions. Fill with pattern.

VARIATIONS

If you want a different brick pattern, you can use the file Flemish.Psd on the *Photoshop Textures Magic* CD-ROM. Follow the original instructions starting with Step 6. This pattern is called a Flemish Bond by bricklayers.

To add other colors to the brick, airbrush the brick color map rather than generating it using the Pointillize filter. I used the colors in the Bricks.Act file on the *Photoshop Textures Magic* CD-ROM. ■

Brocades are two-toned fabrics in which the pattern and toning occur in the weave structure rather than in the color of the threads used. Brocades are elegant and change depending upon the play of light. Here is a computer-generated technique that retains the optical magic of a woven brocade.

1 Create a new file. Mine is 300×300 pixels. Switch to default colors. Select Filter➡Render➡Clouds. You can press (Command-F) [Control-F] to repeat the filter until you like the general mix of black-and-white.

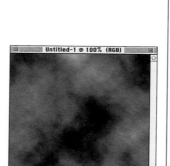

2 Select Image➡Adjust➡Posterize. The number of levels should be an even number from 4–10. I chose 6 levels because that seemed most attractive when I tried out a variety of levels on this texture.

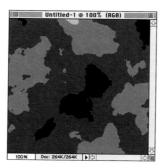

3 To remove the jagged edges (to get spots or dots), you need to apply Filter➡Blur➡Gaussian Blur. I used a Radius of 5. Blur the image until you almost cannot distinguish the separate colors.

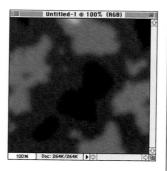

4 Select Image➡Adjust➡Posterize again. Use the same number of Levels as before. Notice how much rounder the shapes have become.

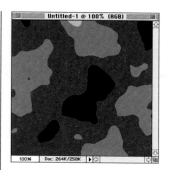

5 Double-click the Magic Wand tool and set the Tolerance to 0. Turn Anti-aliased on. Click in the darkest spot in the image. Choose Select➡Similar. Fill the selection with foreground color (black).

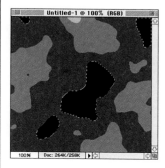

6 Click inside of the next-darkest area (it should surround your last selection). Choose Select➡Similar. Fill the selection with background color (white).

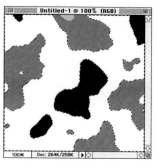

7 Repeat Steps 5 and 6 for all of the remaining values in the image. There may not be six values even if you selected six levels, so it is diffi-cult to predict how many times you need to do this. The object of this is to make the image black-and-white but still preserve the dots and spots. Deselect.

47

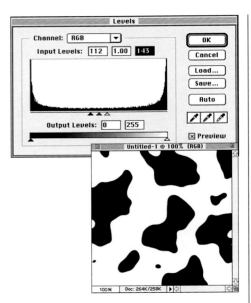

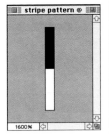

8 Select Filter➡Blur➡Gaussian Blur. I used a Radius of 3.5. Anything from 2–5 should be okay as long as you can see the image detail when the image is blurred. You do need to use a Radius of at least 1 in order to smooth the edges of the shapes. Select Image➡Adjust➡ Levels, and drag the black and white Input sliders toward the center of the histogram. They should line up close to one another at a position where the shape edges are smooth.

9 Select➡All. Define the pattern. Create a new file that is three times the size of the original. Fill with pattern. This image is not seamless, but because it is black-and-white (and will remain two-toned), it does not matter. The straight edges will actually look good.

10 Make the Channels palette active. Create a new channel (Channel #4). Fill with pattern. This is the same pattern that is in the RGB channel.

11 To create the pattern that produces the brocade, create a new file 1 pixel wide × 10 pixels high. Using the Pencil tool and the 1-pixel brush, color the first five pixels of the file black.

12 Select➡All. Define the pattern. Make the large, pattern-filled brocade image active. Return to the composite channel. Load the selection in Channel #4. Fill with pattern. Do not deselect.

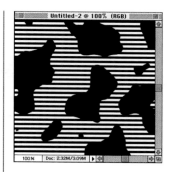

13 Make the stripe pattern file active. Select Image➡Rotate Canvas➡90° CW. Select➡All. Define the pattern. Make the large brocade image active. Reverse the selection (Select➡Inverse). Fill with pattern. Drop the selection.

14 Select Filter➡Blur➡Gaussian Blur. I used a Radius of 2. You just need to blur the pattern a little bit before you emboss it.

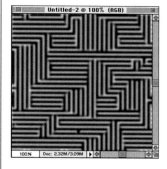

15 Choose Filter➡Stylize➡Emboss (Angle: 136°, Height: 3 pixels, Amount: 100).

16 You can now color the texture. Create an adjustment layer for Hue/Saturation. Click the Colorize button and pick any color that you like. I used settings of −131 for Hue, 37 for Saturation, and −12 for Lightness.

17 Double-click the rectangular Marquee and set a fixed size to the size of the original image (mine is 300×300 pixels). Drag the Marquee into the center of the image. It does not need to be exactly the center but it does need to be close to the center. Make the Background layer active. Define the pattern. Create a new file of the desired size (or simply crop the pattern image and save the tile for later use). If you create a new file, fill with pattern. The 300-pixel selection is seamless—which it would not have been, because of the embossing, if you had built it all in the original 300-pixel square image.

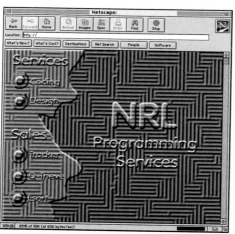

VARIATIONS

If you want a pattern that is seamless before you add the brocade, after Step 9, select Filter➡Other➡Offset (Wrap Around). Make the Horizontal and Vertical distances one-half of the image dimensions. Select Filter➡Blur➡Gaussian Blur. Apply as large a blur as you can without losing any shapes. I used a Radius of 7. Select Image➡Adjust➡Levels and adjust the histogram exactly as you did in Step 8. Select and define a center tile as you did in Step 17. Deselect. Fill with pattern. This time, it is seamless. You can proceed with the original instructions—or create a Dalmatian, or a spotted cow.

To add an actual tone on tone after Step 16, make the Background layer active. Load the selection in Channel #4. Create an adjustment layer for Levels (this one will use the selection). Drag the gamma Input slider to the right or left to make the selection darker or lighter. Proceed with Step 17. ■

A bumpy texture almost sounds redundant. You need to remember, however, that "smooth" is also a texture. A "bumpy" texture is the basic building block for using textures in Photoshop. In its simplest form, you can create a bumpy surface by applying the Add Noise filter to an empty image, embossing the image, and then blurring it a tiny bit.

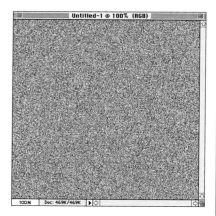

1 Create a new file. Mine is 400×400 pixels. Select Filter➡ Noise➡Add Noise. Add Noise is one of the few filters that works in a totally white image. You can use any settings you want. I used an Amount of 300, a Gaussian distribution, and Monochromatic off. A larger setting results in stronger texture, whereas a lower setting can produce a slight texture. The amount of noise needed depends on the resolution of your finished image. An image that is to be printed at a 150-line screen needs more noise than a 72 dpi image of the same dimensions in inches.

2 Apply Filter➡Brush Strokes➡ Sumi-e with a Stroke Width of 10, a Stroke Pressure of 2, and a Contrast of 16. Most of the filters from the Artistic, Brush Strokes, or Sketch categories will also produce interesting textures using this effect.

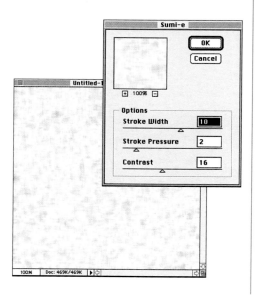

3 Choose Filter➡Stylize➡Emboss. I used an Angle of 130°, a Height of 2 pixels, and an Amount of 100. Select Image➡Adjust➡Desaturate to remove the "odd" colors left by the Emboss filter. If the embossed surface looks too harsh, apply Filter➡Blur➡Gaussian Blur. Use a low setting of 0.3 to 1.5. You can always blur your image more—if you over-blur, the only way to fix it is to apply the Emboss filter again.

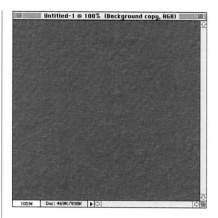

4 Create Layer 0. Create a new Background layer.

5 Switch the foreground color to whichever color you want to use for the base. I selected a medium blue. Fill the Background layer with the foreground color.

6 Make Layer 0 active. Change the blending mode to Hard Light.

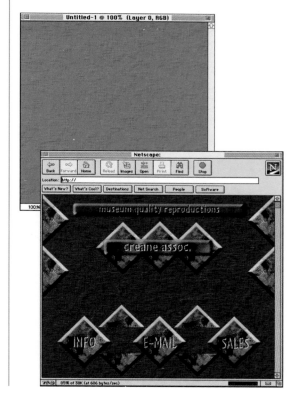

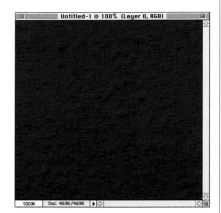

VARIATIONS

Texture Variations

If you want a deeper image, change the blending mode to Color Burn.

Or change the blending mode to Multiply.

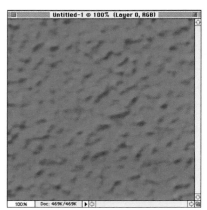

To add softness, make Layer 0 active. Choose Image➡Adjust➡ Auto Levels. Select Filter➡Blur➡ Gaussian Blur. I used a Radius of 3.2.

Then, you can make a double texture. Make the Background layer active. Select Filter➡Noise➡Add Noise. I used an Amount of 40.

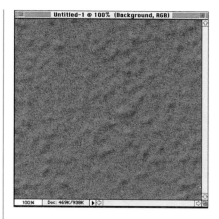

Try applying a filter to the Background layer. I used Filter➡Brush Strokes➡Ink Outlines with a Stroke Length of 4, a Dark Intensity of 20, and a Light Intensity of 10.

Now, try Filter➡Stylize➡Emboss. I used an Angle of 130°, a Height of 2, and an Amount of 100. Then, create a Hue/Saturation adjustment layer at the top of the Layer list. I selected the Colorize flag and moved the Hue to a gold, lowered the Saturation, and lightened the image a bit. A close-up of the texture looks like a dry loofa sponge.

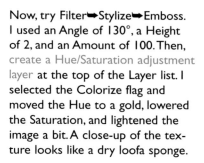
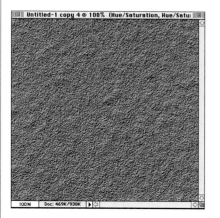

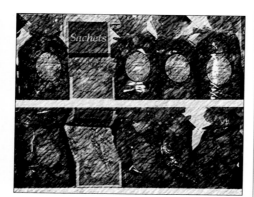

Try varying the type of noise (Filter➡Artistic➡Film Grain and Filter➡Texture➡Grain make wonderful noisy textures), and vary the amount of noise as well.

Textured Photos

You can add wonderful textures to photographs using this effect. Open the photo that you want to texture. Create a new file that is the same size as the photo. In the new file, complete Steps 1, 2, and 3 from the original instructions. Make the photo active. Drag and drop the photo centered into the texture image. Change the blending mode to Hard Light. You could instead drag the texture on top of the photo. If you do, select Overlay or Soft Light as the blending mode.

You get a slightly different application of texture if you use a layer mask for the texture. In the photo, create Layer 0. Create a new Background layer. Make Layer 0 active. Create a layer mask. Complete Steps 1 through 3 of the original instructions in this layer mask. Select Image➡Adjust➡Levels and move the Gamma slider until you are satisfied with the amount of texture in the image. Making the layer mask darker will remove more of the original image from view, whereas making it lighter will keep more of the original image. ■

Did you ever sit on a cane chair as a child and press your hand into the open spaces of the weave? If you pressed hard enough, you picked up a lovely pattern. The interlacing always fascinated me, but I never had the patience to construct my own chair seats. Now, neither of us needs patience—just these instructions.

1 When a craftsperson creates a chair, every portion of the seat needs to be woven. On the computer, you only need to create one "intersection." Create a new file 60×60 pixels. View the image at 500% (or the largest amount that will fit on your screen) by dragging the slider on the Navigator palette. Make the window a little bit larger than the image. Turn on the Rulers (Command-R)[Control-R]. To make the ruler units appear in pixels, double-click on one of the rulers. The Units & Rulers Preferences dialog appears. Change the units to pixels.

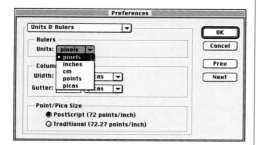

2 Add a vertical and horizontal guide at the center mark on both rulers (30 pixels). This guide is for reference only. The next set of guides determines where the cane "fibers" will be. They need to be created at the center of the lines that you will draw. Add vertical and horizontal guides at 24 and 36 pixels on both rulers.

3 Switch to default colors. Double-click the Line tool. Set the Mode to Normal, Opacity to 100%, Line width to 8, and Anti-aliased off. Do not select Arrowheads. Create a new layer. Place the cursor on the 24-pixel vertical guide *above* the image, and drag a line along the guide to a point *below* the image (this ensures that the line traverses the entire image). Press the Shift key as you drag to constrain the line vertically.

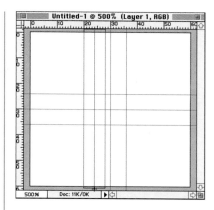

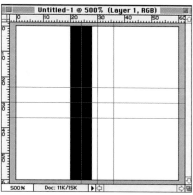

4 Select Filter➡Stylize➡Find Edges. This step allows you to color the cane later.

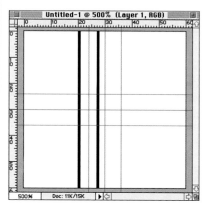

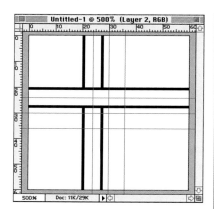

5 Create a new layer. Place your cursor on the 24-pixel horizontal guide at the left outside the image and drag a line to the right along the guide. Press the Shift key as you drag to constrain the line horizontally. Select Filter➡Stylize➡Find Edges.

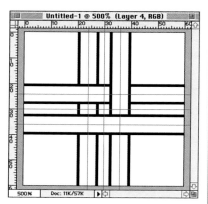

6 Create a new layer. Place your cursor on the 36-pixel vertical guide at the top outside the image and drag a line to the bottom along the guide. Press the Shift key as you drag to constrain the line vertically. Select Filter➡Stylize➡Find Edges. Create a new layer. Draw a line along the 36-pixel horizontal guide. Select Filter➡Stylize➡Find Edges.

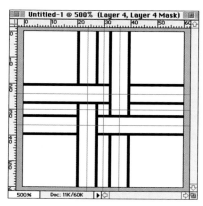

7 Whoops! Weaving is supposed to go over-and-under, and this last line goes over and over. Not to worry. Create a layer mask. Your foreground color should still be black. Switch the foreground color to black if it is not. Place the cursor on the 24-pixel vertical guide line and drag a line on the mask so that it covers the horizontal line that crosses it. The cane line looks as though it has been woven "under." Turn off the Rulers (Command-R) [Control-R].

8 This is the cane repeat unit. Click on the thumbnail for Layer 4 so that the mask is no longer active. Make the Background layer invisible. Select➟All. Define the pattern.

9 Create a new file 360×360 pixels. (I know that is an unusual file size—however, it is an *even* multiple of the repeat tile size of 60 pixels.) Create a new layer. Fill the new image with the pattern. Notice, please, that I have been careful to have you create the pattern so that it preserves transparency. By turning off the Background layer, you have a pattern that can layer over other images. By filling a *layer* in the new image, you continue to keep open the pattern options.

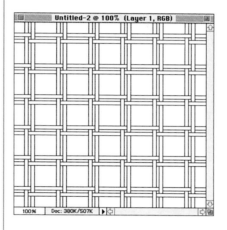

10 The image is useful as it is now, but the beauty of caning is that there is a diagonal element as well. Duplicate Layer 1. Select Layer➟Transform➟Numeric (Shift-Command-T)[Shift-Control-T]. Set the Angle to 45°.

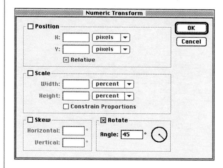

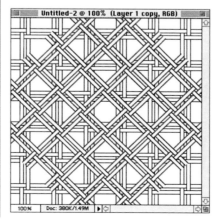

61

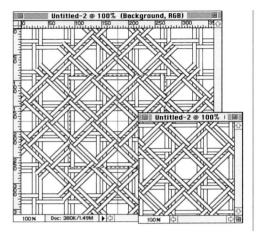

11 That is much more interesting. You need to define a new repeat pattern from this. Double-click the rectangular Marquee tool. Set a fixed size to 180×180 pixels (three times the size of the original tile). Turn on the Rulers (Command-R) [Control-R]. Add a vertical and horizontal guide at the 180 pixel mark on both rulers (this is the exact center of the image). Place your cursor at the intersection of the two guides, press the (Option)[Alt] key and click the mouse button. The fixed size selection rectangle is perfectly centered. Select Image➡ Crop to crop to the dimensions of the Marquee.

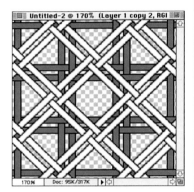

12 Now you can color the weave. "Natural" cane chairs are usually some brownish color. Switch the foreground color to your "cane" color. I selected RGB: 181, 99, 50. Make Layer 1 active. Duplicate Layer 1 (Layer 1 copy 2). Turn on Preserve Transparency. Fill with foreground color. Position the layer below Layer 1. Make Layer 1 active. Change the blending mode to Multiply. Now you can see the black outlines around the weave.

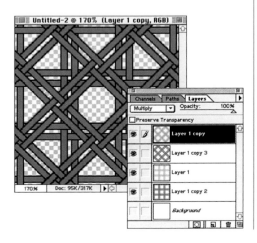

13 Make Layer 1 copy active. Duplicate Layer 1 copy (Layer 1 copy 3). Turn on Preserve Transparency. Fill with foreground color. Position the layer below Layer 1 copy. Make Layer 1 copy active. Change the blending mode to Multiply.

14 Make the Background layer invisible. Select➡All. Define the pattern. Create a new file. Mine is 750 pixels square. Create a new layer. Fill with pattern. You have created a complex (though technically impossible) weave. However, only a weaver with very good eyesight would realize that the weave structure on this does not work.

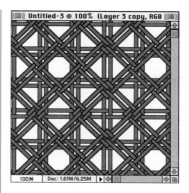

15 Make the Background layer active. Switch the foreground color to a light neutral "ground" color. Fill with foreground color (or create a simple grainy texture like the ones in the effect). Make Layer 1 active. Create a dark glow to shadow the layer. Duplicate Layer 1. Position the new layer below Layer 1. Turn on Preserve Transparency. Switch to default colors. Fill with foreground color. Turn off Preserve Transparency. Select Filter➡Blur➡Gaussian Blur (2.0).

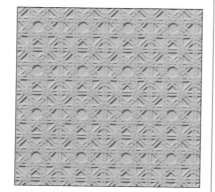

VARIATIONS

This effect makes a wonderful embossed texture. Complete the original instructions through Step 14. Make the Background layer active. Change the foreground color to your desired color. I used RGB: 219, 201, 166. Fill with foreground color. Make Layer 1 active. Choose Filter➡Stylize➡Emboss (Angle: 118°, Height: 3 pixels, Amount: 100). Select Image➡ Adjust➡Desaturate (Shift-Command-U)[Shift-Control-U]. Change the blending mode to Hard Light. Select Filter➡Blur➡ Gaussian Blur. I used a Radius of 2.0, but you can increase the Radius to soften the effect (or use a smaller Radius if you like a sharper image).

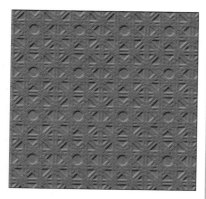

To add a two-toned look to the embossing you just did, redefine (if it is not the current pattern) the cane tile as a pattern as you did in Step 14. Create a new layer in the embossed image. Position the layer below the Hard Light layer. Fill with pattern. Turn on Preserve Transparency. Switch the foreground color to the desired color. I used RGB: 214, 31, 24. Fill with foreground color. Reduce the layer opacity as desired. I set it to 23%.

Then, if you want embossing that sets the cane into the background rather than out of the background, make the Hard Light layer active. Invert the image (Command-I) [Control-I]. (You could also emboss the layer at an Angle of –67° if you were starting over). Shown here is the image with the second color layer (created in Variation 2) turned off. ■

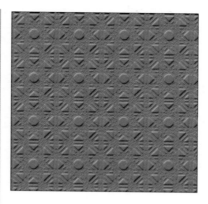

carpet

I've always loved the way carpet squishes beneath my feet. The play of light on carpet fibers is fascinating. There is hidden complexity in the very simplest of structures if you take the time to notice it. This effect recreates a slightly shaggy rug—almost a cut Berber texture. It's a comfortable carpet—you'd notice spilled wine, but pretzel crumbs just sink right in.

1 Create a new file. Mine is 400×400 pixels. Select Filter➡ Noise➡Add Noise (Distribution: Gaussian, Monochromatic Off). I used an Amount of 43. The noise needs to be kept fairly light for the effect to work properly.

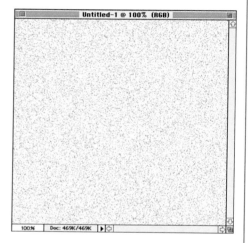

2 Select Filter➡Brush Strokes➡ Ink Outlines. I used a Stroke Length of 4, a Dark Intensity of 20, and a Light Intensity of 10. The Stroke Length setting is the important one. Longer should be okay, but too short a Stroke Length makes the texture too dense and black.

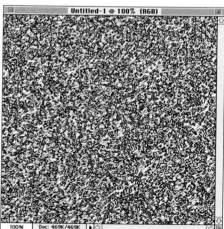

3 Choose Image➥Adjust➥Curves (Command-M)[Control-M]. Make scribbles with the Pencil tool in two or more of the image's color channels. The colors do not matter. What matters is the shape of the texture that appears. You need to create a texture with interesting areas in it, but one which still contains a lot of white space. I drew in the Red and Green channels and left the Blue channel alone. Click OK when you have finished playing with the Curves and return to the main image. Save the file as Cmap.Psd.

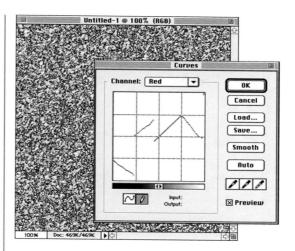

4 Create a new file the same size as the first. Change the foreground color to neutral gray (RGB: 128, 128, 128). Fill with foreground color. Select Filter➥Pixelate➥Pointillize (8). This is the start of the surface map.

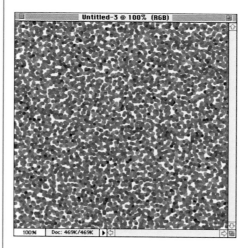

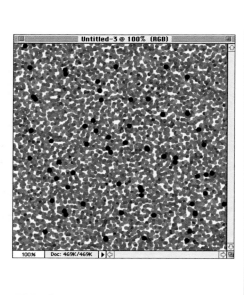

5 Switch to default colors. Double-click the Paintbrush tool. The Mode should be Normal and the opacity 100%. Select a small hard brush (the fourth one of the top row is a good size match to the result of the Pointillize filter). Spatter approximately 50 drops of "paint" all over the image (for a 400-pixel image). Make sure that they are not evenly distributed. Add some additional spots near ones that are already in the image (perhaps another 10). These spots will become the areas of highlight and shadow that give the carpet some interest.

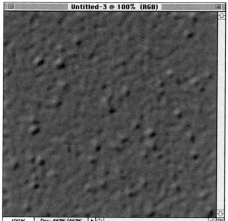

6 Select Filter➡Blur➡Gaussian Blur (4.1). Choose Filter➡Stylize➡Emboss (Angle: 130°, Height: 3 pixels). Use an Amount of 80–130. I chose an Amount of 116. Select Image➡Adjust➡Desaturate (Shift-Command-U)[Shift-Control-U]. The Desaturate command removes the color from the image so that it does not detract from the embossing that you just did.

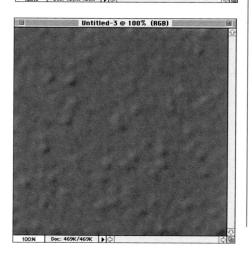

7 Select Filter➡Blur➡Gaussian Blur (4.1) again. The surface map should look very shiny and almost smooth except for the larger bumps where you painted on the Pointillize filter.

68

8 Create a Hue/Saturation adjustment layer. Click the Colorize button. Set the Hue to something "natural"—in the earth tones—and turn the saturation way down. The image should be fairly light.

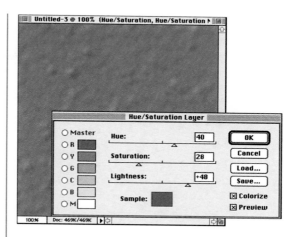

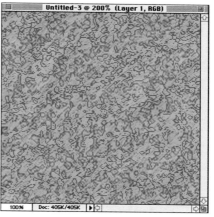

9 Drag and drop centered the Cmap.Psd image into the surface map image. It should be the top layer. Change the blending mode to Color Burn and reduce the layer opacity to approximately 60%.

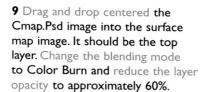

10 Make the Background layer active. Duplicate the Background layer. Position the duplicate layer at the top of the Layers list. Change the blending mode to Hard Light.

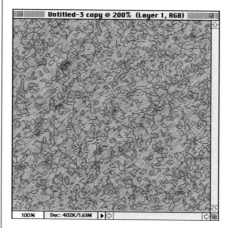

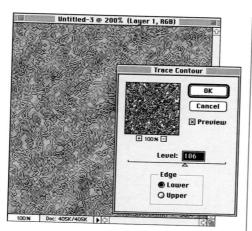

11 Make Layer 1 active. Select Filter➡Stylize➡Trace Contour. I used a lower edge of 106. This filter adds back some of the detail bleached out by the Hard Light and Color Burn modes. This image will become the "fuzz" on the carpet.

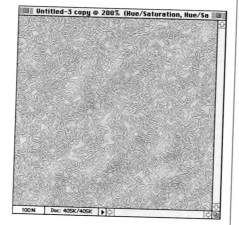

12 Flatten the image (or select Image➡Duplicate (Merged Layers only) if you want to keep a copy of your work editable). Create a Hue/Saturation adjustment layer. Click the Colorize button. Select the color that you want your carpet to be. I stayed with the neutral earth tones.

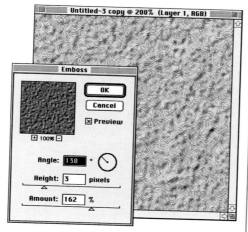

13 Create a new layer. Change the foreground color to neutral gray (RGB: 128, 128, 128). Fill the image with the foreground color. Select Filter➡Noise➡Add Noise (Distribution: Gaussian, Monochromatic). I used an Amount of 42. Select Filter➡Blur➡Gaussian Blur (0.9). Choose Filter➡Stylize➡Emboss (Angle: 138°, Height: 3 pixels, Amount: 162). Change the blending mode to Hard Light. Select Filter➡Blur➡Gaussian Blur (0.7) if the shag is too sharp.

VARIATIONS

If you want to add a little bit more color interest, double-click the Hue/Saturation adjustment layer (if you did not flatten the image and you have more than one, use the highest one) and remove the Colorize flag. Move the Hue slider until you find a combination that you like. I used Hue: +32, Saturation: −34: and Lightness: +46. Of course, your results depend upon your starting colors.

To create a two-toned carpet, create a Curves adjustment layer below the Hue/Saturation adjustment layer. Reverse some of the channel values or draw in the channel grid. Shown is the only change that I made to the Curves. Depending upon the colors in your image, you may need to make more substantial changes to the image Curves.

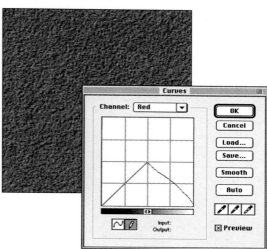

You can also make a mostly seamless repeat from this texture with no extra work. Generally, the pattern only leaves the type of seams that you would see from a vacuum cleaner. ■

Creating ceramic tiles can really spark your creativity. It is easy and breezy, and works because of a trick—you develop little, diagonally colored blocks that can be arranged in a myriad of ways.

1 Create a new file. The file size can be any size, but for right now, it should be a perfect square. Mine is 50×50 pixels (so the result will print at approximately six to the inch). You need to select two colors—one for the tile grout and one to "influence" the color of the tile. Switch the foreground color to your grout color. Switch the background color to the influence color. I selected a light gray for the grout, and a soft lilac for the influence. Fill with background color.

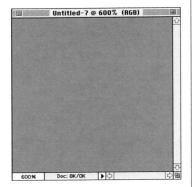

2 Apply Filter➡Texture➡Grain (Grain Type: Clumped). I used an Intensity of 40 and a Contrast of 50.

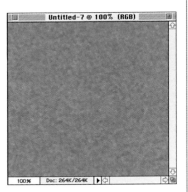

3 Select Filter➡Texture➡Stained Glass (Cell Size: 50, Light Intensity: 0). I used a Border Thickness of 4. You must use a cell size of 50 (the maximum) in order for this trick to work. I recommend a light intensity of 0, as the lighting play from this filter is not very attractive at the settings used here. Notice how the original influence color has changed. The color results from the Stained Glass filter are not totally

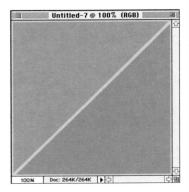

predictable, but they are based on the colors found in the image. The border thickness uses the foreground color to set the grout.

4 Next, you need to make the tile look beveled. Select➥All. Select➥ Modify➥Border. The amount of the border that you should select depends on your image size. For the 50-pixel image, I selected a border of 8 pixels (64 pixels is the maximum possible).

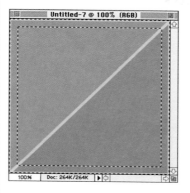

5 Switch to default colors. Create a new layer. Fill the border selection with foreground color. Deselect. Reduce the layer opacity. I used an opacity of 43%. You can define this tile as a pattern and use it as is, but there is a lot more that you can do in addition to just repeating it.

6 Flatten the image. Select➥All and copy the image to the clipboard. Create a new file that is twice the dimensions of the copy on the clipboard. Make the tile seamless using the Mosaic method.

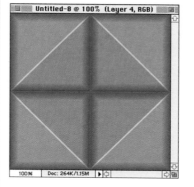

73

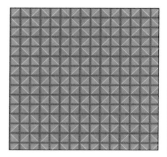

7 Select→All. Define the pattern. Create a new file. Mine is 750×750 pixels. Fill with pattern.

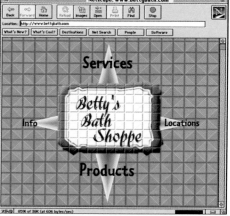

VARIATIONS

If you want a two-toned tile with more contrast in the halves, use the Add Noise filter in Step 2 instead of the Grain filter. The more noise that you add, the greater the variation possible in the two halves of the tile. This image used RGB: 174, 201, 97 and a noise amount of 29...

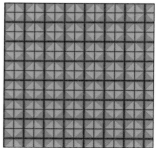

...and this one used a noise amount of 300.

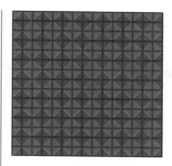

To vary the repeat a bit, you can use a pinwheel method of making the image seamless. Create a new file twice the dimensions of the original. Make the pattern seamless using the Mosaic method with these exceptions: Copy the upper-left tile to the upper-right corner, and instead of flipping it horizontally, select Layer➥Transform➥Rotate 90° CCW. Copy this rotated image (using the fixed size Marquee) and paste it into the bottom-right corner. Select Layer➥Transform➥ Rotate 90° CCW. Copy this and paste it into the bottom-left corner. Select Layer➥Transform➥Rotate 90° CCW. Select➥All. Define the pattern. Create a new file. Fill with pattern.

You can mix and match tiles that were created separately using the Mosaic or Pinwheel repeat method.

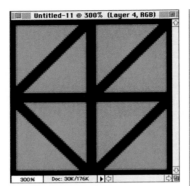

To create a tile with no color variation, do not add a noise filter in
Step 2. You must use a Border
Thickness greater than 1 if you
want a decent result. You also need
to use a color that contrasts with
your fill as the foreground color. I
used a Border Thickness of 8 and a
Light Intensity of 1 (just a gentle
light for the sake of variation). I also
used the Mosaic method to make
the pattern seamless, but I left the
upper-right corner as a repeat of
the upper-left corner. This breaks
the pattern and creates even more
interest.

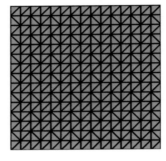

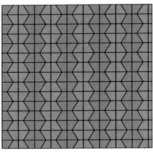

You can also create rectangular tiles
that form hexagonal shapes. Create
a new file 81 pixels wide × 50 pixels high. Complete the original
steps. Make the pattern seamless
using the Mosaic method.

If you want to mix sizes of tiles, follow the original steps for each size. The sizes should be multiples of one another. Here, I used a 150-pixel tile surrounded by 50-pixel tiles. ■

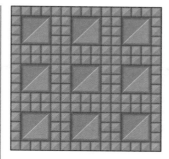

Whether you see a circle as a geo-metric object or a metaphor for life, you see circles everywhere. They have been used as symbols since prehistoric times. This pattern uses circles within circles to create an embossed repeat, suitable for a background or a texture wrap of a three-dimensional object. It can be as subtle or as flashy as you want.

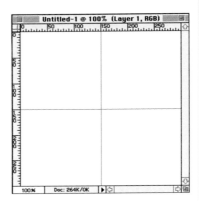

1 Create a new file. Use an even number of pixels. Mine is 300×300 pixels. Create a new layer. Switch to default colors. Turn on the Rulers (Command-R)[Control-R]. Add a vertical guide in the center of the image. Add a horizontal guide at the mid-point of the side ruler.

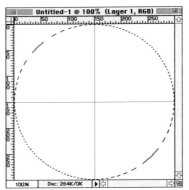

2 Double-click the Marquee tool to open the Marquee Options dialog box. Select elliptical as the Shape. Set a fixed size for the Marquee tool of 300×300 pixels (or the size of your image). Place the cursor at the intersection of the horizontal and vertical guides. Press the (Option)[Alt] key and click with the mouse. This leaves a perfect circle selected at the exact center of the image.

3 Select Edit➥Stroke. Set the Stroke width to 3 pixels and the Location to Inside. Make sure that the opacity is 100% and the Mode is Normal. Deselect.

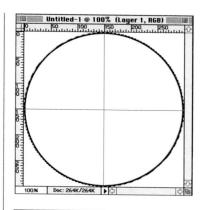

4 Set a fixed size for the elliptical Marquee tool of 200×200 pixels (or the same general fraction of your image). Place the cursor at the intersection of the horizontal and vertical guides. Press the (Option) [Alt] key and click with the mouse.

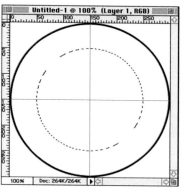

5 Choose Edit➥Stroke with the same settings used in Step 3. Deselect.

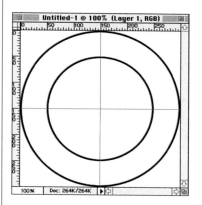

79

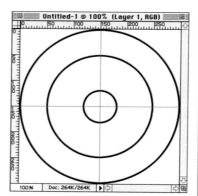

6 Set a fixed size for the elliptical Marquee tool of 65×65 pixels (or the same general fraction of your image). Place the cursor at the intersection of the horizontal and vertical guides. Press the (Option) [Alt] key and click with the mouse. Choose Edit➡Stroke with the same settings as before. Deselect.

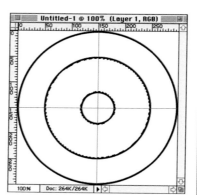

7 Double-click the Magic Wand tool and set the Tolerance to 10 and Anti-aliased on. Click inside of the middle circle to select it.

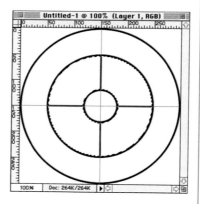

8 Double-click the Line tool. Set the Line Width to 3 and Anti-aliased on. Do not use arrowheads. Place the cursor at the intersection of the two guidelines, and draw a straight line up to the top of the image. Because of the selection Marquee, the line is only drawn in the middle circle. Repeat for straight lines going down, left, and right from the center.

9 You next need to draw lines going diagonally. Again, place your cursor at the center of the image. This time, because you have no diagonal guides to follow, press the Shift key as you drag a line diagonally from the center. The Shift key will constrain it to a 45° angle. Place all four diagonal lines. It is critical that you start from the exact center of the image. You will know that the cursor is correctly positioned when it turns a different color as it is situated over the intersection of the guides. Turn off the Rulers (Command-R)[Control-R]. Hide the guides (Command-;)[Control-;]. Deselect.

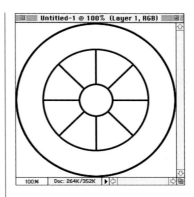

10 Duplicate Layer 1. Select Filter➡Other➡Offset (Wrap Around). Make the Horizontal and Vertical distances one-half of the image dimensions (150 pixels in each direction).

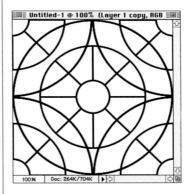

11 Make Layer 1 active. Select Layer➡Free Transform (Command-T) [Control-T]. Press the Shift and (Option)[Alt] key and drag the upper-right corner point until it touches the lower portion of the diagonal line in the upper-right of the image (as shown in the figure). Press the (Return)[Enter] key to execute the transformation.

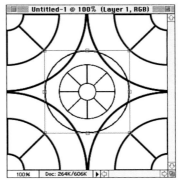

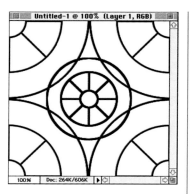

12 Load the transparency selection of Layer 1. **Select Edit➡Stroke, 2 pixels, Center.** This thickens the lines that were scaled. Deselect.

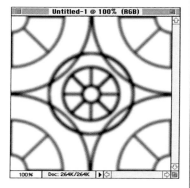

13 Flatten the image. **Select Filter➡Blur➡Gaussian Blur (2.5).**

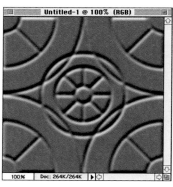

14 Choose **Filter➡Stylize➡Emboss (Angle: −67°, Height: 3 pixels, Amount: 100).** If you change these settings, watch the preview carefully. At a number of different angles, some of the straight or diagonal lines are completely lost.

15 Create an adjustment layer for Hue/Saturation. Click Colorize. Change to the desired color. I set a Hue of −68, Saturation of 28, and lightness of +41.

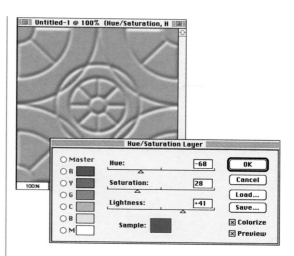

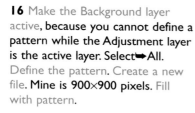

16 Make the Background layer active, because you cannot define a pattern while the Adjustment layer is the active layer. Select➡All. Define the pattern. Create a new file. Mine is 900×900 pixels. Fill with pattern.

VARIATIONS

If you want the texture to be raised rather than indented, make the Background layer active. **Invert (Command-I)[Control-I].**

To create a much softer embossing, at the end of Step 15, make the Background layer active. **Select Filter➠Blur➠Gaussian Blur,** and soften as much as you want. I used a Radius of 6.0.

You can also use a multi-colored image on top of the embossed layer. Omit Step 15. Complete Step 16 to give you an image of the desired size. Create a new layer. Switch the foreground and background colors to your desired colors. I used a light yellow and a light lavender. Apply Filter➡ Render➡Clouds. Change the blending mode to Overlay. Apply Filter➡Render➡Difference Clouds several times. I applied the filter three times. ▪

Cobblestones
Lighting Effects
preset

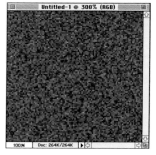

Listen carefully. Can you hear the clip-clop of horses' hooves as they trot down this cobblestone road?

1 Create a new file. Mine is 600×400 pixels. Switch the foreground color to a medium gray or whatever color you want to use for the mortar that holds the cobblestones in place. (The original mortar was probably a light color, but the cobblestone streets in Olde Philadelphia are certainly not light anymore!) I used RGB: 115, 111, 107. Fill with foreground color.

2 Select Filter➥Noise➥Add Noise (Amount: 20, Distribution: Gaussian, Monochromatic). The Amount needs to be low enough so that you do not create white pixels. Use my settings this time before you start experimenting with this one.

3 Create a new layer. The cobblestones are created with the Pointillize filter. This filter uses the Background color as the background for the filter, but it uses the colors already in the image to tone to color blobs. Therefore, you need to first select two colors to apply to the layer. I used an olive (RGB: 119, 116, 72) and a brown (RGB: 92, 57, 41).

4 Select Filter➥Render➥Clouds. This varies the tone of the image for the Pointillize filter's color blobs.

5 Switch the background color to a darker gray. I used RGB: 52, 62, 72. This color will be used to add overall background tone to the cobblestones. Select Filter➥ Pixelate➥Pointillize. I used a cell size of 34. The cell size to choose really depends on where you will use the final result. If you are going to print, you need a larger cell size than you would if you are going to display the image at 72 dpi.

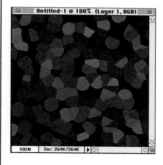

6 Duplicate Layer 1 and rename the layer **Mortar Map**. Make the Mortar Map layer invisible and make Layer 1 active. Rename Layer 1 **color map**. Change the blending mode to **Color Burn** and reduce the layer opacity to **40%**.

87

7 Make the Background layer active. Duplicate the Background layer. Rename the Background copy layer **Texture Map**. Position the layer above the Color Map layer and below the Mortar Map layer.

8 With the Texture Map layer active, choose Filter➡Other➡ Minimum (2 pixels). This filter selects the darker pixels and is a way to increase the size of the noise. Choose Image➡Adjust➡ Auto Levels.

9 Select Filter➡Blur➡Gaussian Blur (1.5) to soften the noise. Choose Filter➡Stylize➡Emboss. I used an Angle of 125°, a Height of 3, and an Amount of 100. Change the blending mode to Hard Light.

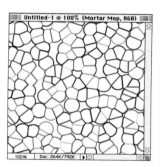

10 Make the Mortar Map layer active. Choose Filter➡Stylize➡Find Edges and then select Image➡ Adjust➡Desaturate. Apply Image➡ Adjust Auto Levels.

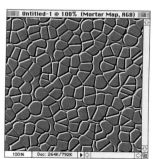

11 Change the blending mode to Hard Light. Apply Filter➡Stylize➡ Emboss. You need to set the angle so that the embossing sinks into the cobblestones. I used the following: Angle: −47°; Height: 3; Amount: 100.

12 The cracks are much too sharp. Apply Filter➡Blur➡Gaussian Blur. You can fiddle with the setting, but somewhere around 1.1 should work.

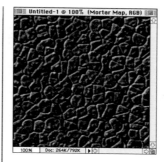

13 The color is still too strong— unless you like colorful cobble- stones. Make the Color Map layer active. Create a Hue/Saturation adjustment layer. Change the set- tings as you prefer. I decreased the Saturation to −42 and the Lightness to −16.

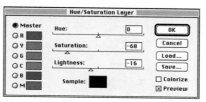

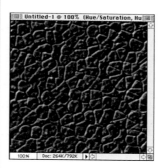

14 Now that you've set the color of the cobblestones, you may want to tweak the Texture Map and Mortar Map layers again. I applied another 1.1 Gaussian Blur to the Mortar Map layer. If you think there is too much shine on the cobble- stones, choose Image➡Adjust Levels and bring the white Output slider to the left until you have removed as much of the highlight- ing as you want.

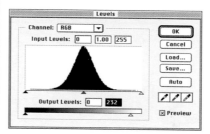

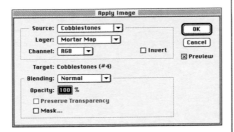

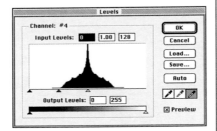

VARIATIONS

If you want a more deeply etched texture, you can apply the Lighting Effects filter to the image. Create a new channel (Channel #4). Select Image➡Apply Image (Source: your image, Layer: Mortar Map, Channel: RGB, Blending: Normal, Opacity: 100%).

Select Image➡Adjust➡Levels. Click to pick up the white point Eye-dropper (the one on the right). Click on one of the areas of neutral gray in the channel. The gray areas turn white.

This enables the cobblestones to come forward and the cracks to recede when you apply the Lighting Effects filter.

Return to the composite channel. Flatten the image. **Choose Filter➡ Render➡Lighting Effects. Use the settings shown, or select the Cobblestones preset in the Lighting folder on the** *Photoshop Textures Magic* **CD-ROM.** ■

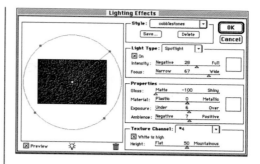

Confetti

This texture looks like a major celebration in process. It is wonderful for any RGB output even if it looks a bit anemic on the printed page. The strong magentas and blues that come from the applied RGB noise do not translate well to print, but this makes a terrific background for a Web page. So grab a bottle of champagne and your party hat!

1 Create a new file. Any size file will work—I started with a file that is 600×400 pixels. Choose Filter➡ Texture➡Grain. Select Clumped as the Grain Type. I use an Intensity setting of 40 and a Contrast of 50.

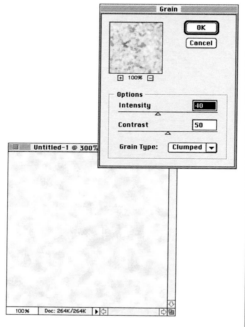

TOOLBOX

Diamond Texture
Lighting Filter
preset

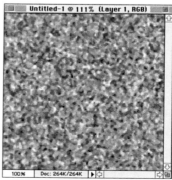

2 Choose Image➡Adjust➡Auto Levels.

3 This is much too dark. Select Filter➡Fade Auto Levels. Decrease the opacity to about 44% and select Hard Light blending mode.

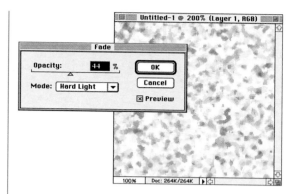

4 Create a new layer. Switch to default colors. Fill the selection with background color. This seems peculiar, but don't do anything to this layer.

5 Duplicate the Background layer. Position the layer at the top of the layer list in the Layers palette.

6 Make the Background copy layer active. Choose Filter➡Blur➡ Gaussian Blur (8.5 pixels). The data in the image becomes so light as to be almost invisible. That's fine—it is still there.

7 Choose Filter➡Stylize➡Find Edges. The data is still too light to see.

93

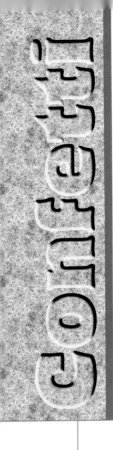

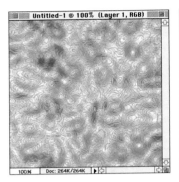

8 Apply Image➞Adjust➞Auto Levels. Finally! An image appears.

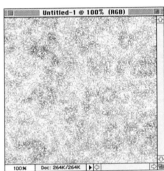

9 Change the blending mode to Dissolve and reduce the layer's opacity until the image looks spattered onto the blank layer beneath. I used an opacity of 60%.

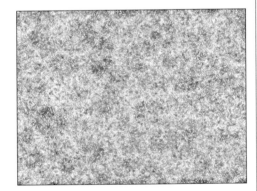

10 Merge Down (Command-E) [Control-E]. Now change the blending mode to Multiply. This keeps the "spots" created by using Dissolve mode, and enables you to change the blending mode as well.

VARIATIONS

Web Patterns

If you want to make a seamless tile for the Web, you need to first decide how big the tile can be. I started with a tile 50×50 pixels. Set the rectangular Marquee to a fixed size of whatever you want your tile size to be. Drag the Marquee around the original image (use the Marquee tool, not the Move tool to drag) until you find a spot that you like. Copy the selected area to the clipboard. Create a new file. Paste the image in from the clipboard. Do not flatten. Select➡All. Define a Pattern. Create a new file at least as large as your Web page to test the pattern. I used 640×480. Fill the selection with pattern. Most areas of the original will tile seamlessly without doing anything to them. If necessary, make the image seamless using the Rubber Stamp method. When you like the results, convert the image to Indexed Color mode, using the Web Palette option. Save the file in GIF format.

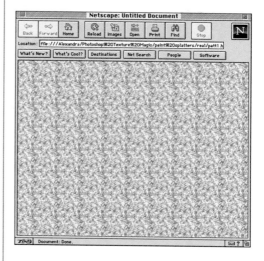

To add some interest to the pattern, use a brick repeat rather than a simple rectangular repeat. Repeat the instructions for the first Web pattern until you have pasted the small pattern into its own file. Again, do not flatten. Choose Image➡Canvas Size. Anchor the image in the upper-center square, and double the original height (I doubled the 50-pixel height to 100 pixels). Duplicate layer 1. Choose Filter➡Other➡Offset. Offset the layer by half of the current height and width of the image (I used an offset of 50 pixels down and 25 pixels right). Wrap around. Select all. Define the pattern. Fill a new selection with the pattern.

A Stronger Celebration

If you want to create a darker version of the original texture, complete Steps 1–10. Create a new layer. Fill with white. Choose Filter➡Texture➡Grain. Select Clumped as the Grain Type. I used an Intensity setting of 40 and a Contrast of 50. Apply Filter➡Stylize➡Find Edges and then apply Filter➡Blur➡Gaussian Blur. Blur the image until the colors merge. I used a Radius of 4.9. Choose Image➡Adjust➡Levels. Move the black Input slider to the left until it reaches the spot where the values in the graph start to sharply increase. Click OK. Change the blending mode to Difference.

A Persian Cloisonné

To produce a delicate texture similar in feel to a Persian garden, repeat the instructions for the previous variation. Instead of creating a blank layer, and filling it with grain, duplicate the Background layer, and apply the Gaussian Blur filter. You do not need to adjust the levels on this variation after you blur it.

Sequined Splendor

You can also get a completely different look by applying the Lighting Effects filter to the original texture through a pattern and doubling it back on itself. Start with the finished image from the original instructions. Flatten the image. Create a new channel. This channel should be solid black. Open the file Diamonds.Psd, choose Select→All, and define the pattern. Click the original texture image to make it active, and fill the blank channel with pattern. Return to the composite channel. Choose Filter→ Render→Lighting Effects. Select the Diamond Texture Lights preset that came from the *Photoshop Textures Magic* CD-ROM. Duplicate the Background layer. Choose Layer→ Transform→Flip Horizontal. Change the blending mode to Multiply. This texture may be too dark and too busy to be a successful Web pattern, but it certainly lights up a night on the town. ■

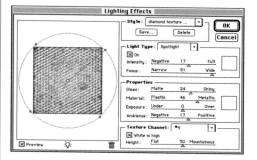

Have you ever stared at a cracker before you ate it? I mean, really looked hard at the texture? It's wonderful! It's lumpy and nicely browned. You can easily create a Saltine-type cracker, or a water-based cracker on the computer. For a large cracker such as a piece of matzo, you can make this seamless using the Brushed Mask method shown in the Photoshop Basics section.

1 Create a new file. Mine is 300×300 pixels. Switch the foreground color to a light cracker-background color. I used RGB: 230, 230, 231. Add the color to your Swatches palette by moving to the first empty spot at the end of the palette. Fill your image with the foreground color.

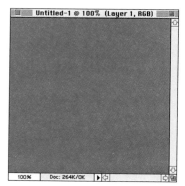

2 Create a new layer (Layer 1). Switch the foreground color to a color suitable for the browned portions of the cracker. I chose RGB: 177, 131, 85. Fill the layer with the foreground color.

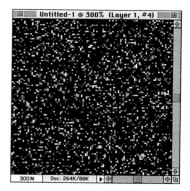

3 Create a new channel (#4). The channel is probably filled with black. This is okay. Apply Filter➡Noise➡ Add Noise (Gaussian). In a channel, the noise already is Monochromatic. I used an Amount of 135.

4 Select Filter➡Pixelate➡ Crystallize (10). The filter is used to help produce the little lumpies in the cracker.

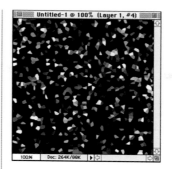

5 Select Image➡Adjust➡ Threshold. I used a Threshold of 100. This makes the lumpies clump together. The dark areas will get "browned" while the white areas will remain the color of the Background layer.

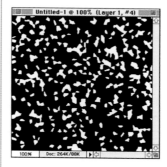

6 Choose Filter➡Blur➡Gaussian Blur. I used a Radius of 5.0. Softening the channel keeps the color from being applied too sharply.

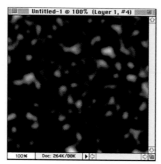

99

7 Load the selection in Channel #4. Return to the composite channel. Make Layer 1 active. Create a layer mask. The mask uses the active selection. Deselect.

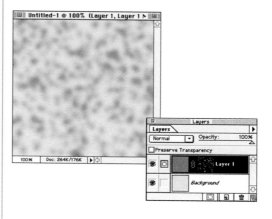

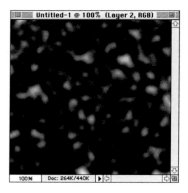

8 So far, you just have a two-toned flat wafer. You need to add some dimension to it. Create a new layer (Layer 2). Select Image➡Apply Image (Channel: #4, Opacity: 100%, Blending: either Normal or Multiply).

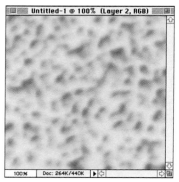

9 Change the blending mode of Layer 2 to Hard Light. Choose Filter➡Stylize➡Emboss (Angle: 127°, Height: 3 pixels, Amount: 64).

10 Switch the foreground color to a darker or different "browned" color. Duplicate Layer 1. Select➡ All. Press the Delete key. This leaves an empty layer that is protected by a layer mask. Select the Airbrush tool with a large brush and a low pressure. Spray a little bit of one or more contrasting colors on this layer. Crunch!

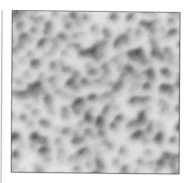

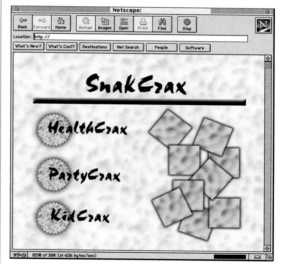

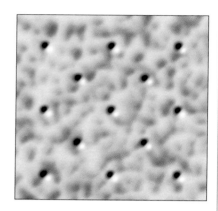

VARIATIONS

If you want to add holes to turn the cracker into a Saltine, turn on the Rulers (Command-R)[Control-R]. Add 3 vertical guides at even intervals. In the 300-pixel square image, I added them at 50, 150, and 250 pixels. Add 3 horizontal guides at the same coordinates on the horizontal axis. Create a new layer (Layer 3). Switch to default colors. Fill Layer 3 with the background color (white). Select the Paintbrush and the 9-pixel hard brush (third from the right in the default Brushes palette). Stamp a brush-stroke down on each grid intersection. Select View➡Clear Guides. Add 2 horizontal guides evenly spaced, and add 2 vertical guides at the same location on the vertical ruler. I added these guides at 100 and 200 pixels. Stamp a brushstroke on these intersections as well. Select Filter➡Blur➡Gaussian Blur (1.3). Change the blending mode to Hard Light. Choose Filter➡Stylize➡Emboss (Angle: −27°, Height: 4 pixels, Amount: 126). You might want to soften the embossing by applying Filter➡Blur➡Gaussian Blur (2.0). You can emboss again at an Angle of 127° if you want to leave light on both sides of the cracker holes.

To add salt to the cracker, create a new channel (#5). It should automatically be filled with black. Select Filter➡Noise➡Add Noise (Distribution: Gaussian, Monochromatic). I used an Amount of 135. Choose Filter➡Pixelate➡Crystallize (3). Select Image➡Adjust Levels and move the Gamma slider (the center one) toward the right until the Gamma point is about 0.53 or the spot at which there is only a small amount of bright white. Load the selection Channel #5. Make the Composite channel active. Make Layer 3 invisible (if you have added holes to the cracker).Make any visible layer active. Merge the visible layers (Shift-Command-E)[Shift-Control-E]. Make Layer 3 visible again. Switch to default colors. Press the Delete key to add a layer of "salt." Deselect. ▪

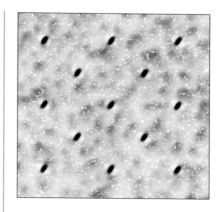

Creased, crumbled, cracked, *crevassed*. This effect fractures your image into organic bits. It makes an effective, soft Web page background when created with a solid color or a muted gradient. This effect also adds a wonderful craquelure accent to an image—in a much more natural manner than the Craquelure filter, and it is excellent as a texture wrap on a 3-D model.

1 Create a new file. Mine is 300×300 pixels. Switch the foreground color to your desired texture color. I selected a light mint-green. Fill with foreground color.

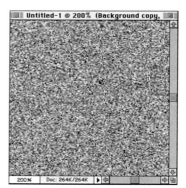

2 Duplicate the Background layer. Select Filter➡Noise➡Add Noise (Distribution: Gaussian, Monochromatic Off). I used an Amount of 135.

3 Apply Filter➡Pixelate➡
Cyrstallize. I used a cell size of 11.
Cell sizes of 8 to 14 give good results. Larger cell sizes produce the
networks seen in "Cobblestones"
(page 86).

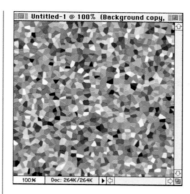

4 Choose Filter➡Stylize➡Find
Edges. These edges form the
shadows in the cracks.

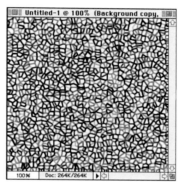

5 Select Image➡Adjust➡
Desaturate (Shift-Command-U)
[Shift-Control-U]. This removes the
odd colors in the image.

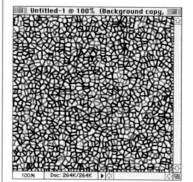

6 Change the blending mode to Hard Light. Now you will be able to evaluate the Emboss filter as you apply it.

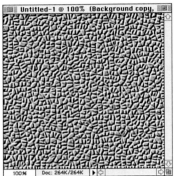

7 Choose Filter➡Stylize➡Emboss (Height: 3 pixels, Amount: 100). I used an Angle of −47° so that the crevasses sink into the texture rather than standing up.

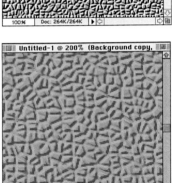

8 The Hard Light mode produces an effect that is much too strong. Reduce the top layer's opacity until you are satisfied with the effect. I used an opacity of 35% because I wanted it to show up in print. If you are using this on a Web page, you can reduce the layer's opacity to as little as 5% and still have a textured background tile.

9 Now, you need to create a seamless tile. Change the blending mode on the Background copy layer back to Normal and set the opacity at 100%. Duplicate the Background copy layer. Make the pattern seamless using the Masked Offset method. Select Layer➡Merge Down (Command-E) [Control-E]. Change the blending mode to Hard Light and reduce the layer opacity back to your desired amount. Select➡All. Define the pattern. Fill an image of the desired size with the pattern (or save the tile as .GIF and use it in a Web page).

VARIATIONS

If you want to texture a photograph, use the photograph as the Background layer. Create an empty layer filled with white in Step 2 instead of duplicating the Background layer. Complete all of the remaining steps until Step 9. This photograph is from the Vivid Details Sampler on the *Photoshop Textures Magic* CD-ROM.

To add a more varied texture to the photograph, duplicate the photograph in Step 2 of the original instructions. Do not apply the Add Noise filter. The texture is not as uniformly crevassed, but the craquelure lines hug the image better. This photograph is also from the Vivid Details Sampler on the *Photoshop Textures Magic* CD-ROM. ∎

Fish scales is one of the classic "building block" patterns that has been used since antiquity. It is a simple geometric form to construct, but can be used as a decoration, texture, or realistic material if you happen to be modeling fish.

1 Create a new file **300** pixels square. You are not limited to that size, but the image does need to be square. Create a new layer (Layer 1). Turn on the Rulers (Command-R) [Control-R]. Add a horizontal and vertical guide at the center point along both rulers. Double-click the Marquee tool. Set the Style to Elliptical and the fixed size to 300×300 pixels (or the size of your image). Place the cursor at the intersection of the two guides. Press the (Option)[Alt] key to create a perfect circle centered in the image.

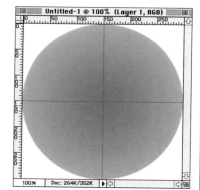

2 Switch the foreground color to the inside color for the fish scale pattern. I used a yellow-green—RGB: 78, 163, 32. Switch the background color to a contrasting color. I used RGB: 202, 215, 65. Double-click the Gradient tool, select the Foreground to Background gradient, and set Dither off. Choose a Radial gradient Type. Place the Gradient cursor at the intersection of the two guides, press the Shift key and the mouse button, and drag the cursor to the edge of the circular selection. Release the mouse button.

3 Select Image➡Adjust➡Posterize. Select 40 levels. This is enough to see real banding in the gradient— which is actually what you are trying to achieve. The banded fish scale pattern is an ancient one in Chinese art.

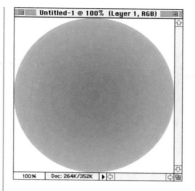

4 Duplicate Layer 1. Deselect. Select Filter➡Other➡Offset (Wrap Around). Make the Horizontal and Vertical distances one-half of the image dimensions (150 pixels for both dimensions in this example).

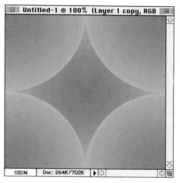

5 Select the rectangular Marquee and set the fixed size to 300 pixels wide × 150 pixels high (or the full width of your image and one-half of the length). In order to create the fish scale illusion, you need to separate the top and bottom halves of Layer 1 copy. Drag the Marquee to select the top half of the image. Select Layer➡New➡Layer Via Cut (Shift-Command-J)[Shift-Control-J]. Position the layer below Layer 1.

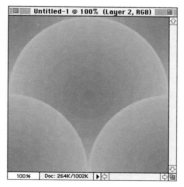

109

6 Select➡All. Define the pattern. Create a new file that is the desired size. Fill the selection with pattern.

VARIATIONS

An infinite number of variations are possible. If you want shadows under the fish scales, you can use a work-around that is fairly easy. A real shadow is difficult to make seamless in this pattern. Complete the example through Step 5. Make Layer 2 invisible, and make Layer 1 active. Load the transparency selection of Layer 1. Create a new layer (Layer 3). Switch to default colors. Fill the selection with background color. Turn on preserve transparency. Choose Select➡Modify➡Border and set a border size of about 26 pixels. Fill the selection with foreground color. This will create the area of darkness at the edges of the fish scale. Duplicate Layer 3. Repeat Steps 4 and 5 with the new layer. Drag each shadow layer above the layer that looks like it. You can see the "shadow" layers in the layers palette—they are Layer 4, Layer 3, and Layer 3 copy. You will not see Layer 4 in the actual image because it is completely covered over.

Change the blending mode to Multiply for each of the shadow layers. Reduce the layer opacity if you want. Continue with Step 6.

You can create a metallic fish scale effect. In Step 2, select the GoldGrad from the *Photoshop Textures Magic* CD-ROM. Fill the circle with a linear gradient dragged across the image from left to right. Choose Select➡Modify➡Contract (10 pixels). Apply the linear gradient, again dragging the cursor from the top of the image to the bottom. Omit Step 3, and proceed with the rest of the original instructions.

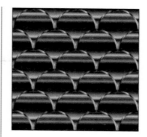

If you are unhappy with the way the Posterize command works in Step 3, use a radial gradient that only contains shades of gray. Switch the foreground color to RGB: 64, 64, 64 and switch the background color to RGB: 192, 192, 192. Use the Fishscale Gradient preset on the *Photoshop Textures Magic* CD-ROM. In Step 4, posterize the circle into 6 levels. The grays will posterize correctly. Work Steps 4 and 5. Select the Paintbrush tool. Pick up the color at the center of each layer (the darkest gray) and paint out the other colors at the bottom of the fish scale. You only need to do this on Layers 1 and 2. Create an adjustment layer for Hue/Saturation. I changed the Hue to −34, the Saturation to 35, and the Lightness to 23. Work Step 6.

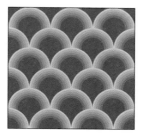

You can also work the original instructions using the Fishscale Gradient preset. If you omit Step 4 and do not posterize, you get a lovely, soft blend. ■

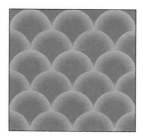

Grass is a challenging texture to design. It has a large number of variables. Do you want to look at the grass up close and personal or from a distance? And what kind of grass—(no, not *that* kind)—do you want to see: grass on a golf course, or the mixture of grass and weeds on an ordinary front lawn (like mine)? The instructions in this effect can work in all situations. This texture will hold its character in print or in multimedia. You just need to decide on the shade of green.

1 Create a new file. You can talk this texture into tiling, so your file can be either full-size or tile-size. Mine is 400×400 pixels. Switch the foreground color to the desired shade of green. I used RGB: 0, 112, 54. Fill with foreground color. Select Filter➠Noise➠Add Noise (Distribution: Gaussian, Monochromatic). I used an Amount of 29. You need to keep the Amount low enough to not place white pixels in the image.

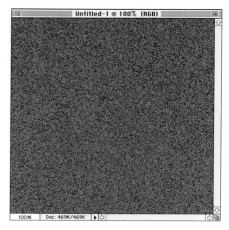

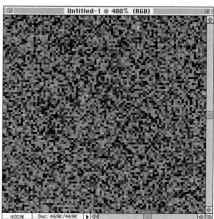

2 Apply Filter➠Texture➠Grain (Grain Type: Regular). I used an Intensity of 40 and a Contrast of 50. This adds a small amount of contrasting (but related) pixels— not the RGB "primary" noise of the Add Noise filter.

3 Apply Filter➡Texture➡Grain (Grain Type: Clumped). I used an Intensity of 40 and a Contrast of 50. This further helps to create a "grassy" base.

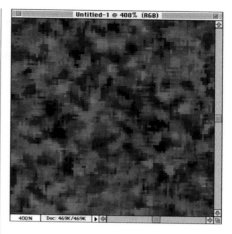

4 Select Filter➡Brush Strokes➡ Spatter. I used a Spray Radius of 10 and a Smoothness of 5. This makes a very paint-like grass texture.

5 Duplicate the Background layer.

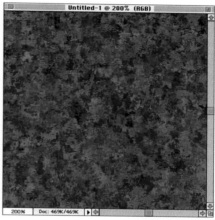

6 Choose Filter➡Blur➡Motion Blur. Pick an Angle that is just a little bit away from 90° and a short Distance. I used an Angle of –74° and a Distance of 8 pixels. This motion blur actually forms the grass blades.

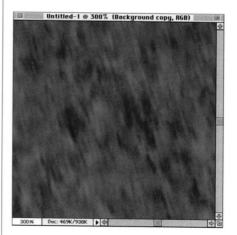

113

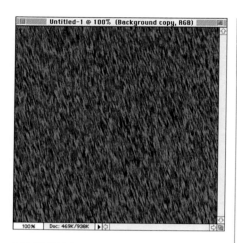

7 The grass needs to be further defined. Select Filter➡Sharpen➡ Unsharp Mask (Amount: 450, Radius: 1.5, Threshold: 0). As in so many of these effects, I chose settings that work for the textures, but are preposterous for prepress use.

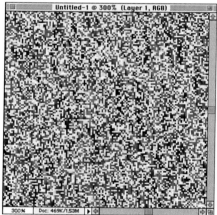

8 Most lawns contain some brown—if not dead spots, then old crabgrass, thatch, or just plain dirt as an underpainting. Create a new layer. Switch the background color to white. Fill with background color. Select Filter➡Noise➡Add Noise (Distribution: Gaussian, Monochromatic). I used an Amount of 29. Double-click the Magic Wand tool and set the Tolerance to 0, Anti-alias off, and no feather. Magnify the layer so that you can see to click on a white pixel. Select➡Similar. Press the Delete key. This leaves only the noise that was on the layer.

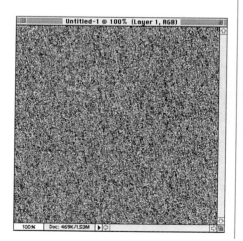

9 Turn on Preserve Transparency. Switch the foreground color to a brown dirt color. I used RGB: 154, 105, 22. Press Shift-Delete to show the Fill dialog box. Fill the layer with foreground color at 100% Opacity in Color mode. Color mode keeps the variation in the value of the noise that is in the layer.

10 Turn off Preserve Transparency. Choose Filter➥Blur➥Motion Blur. Use the same settings as before, or vary the angle a little bit.

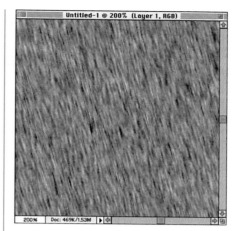

11 Select Image➥Adjust➥Auto Levels.

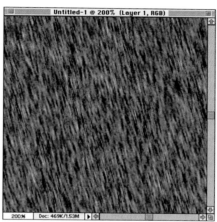

12 You can remove some of the levels adjustment that you just added if the image is too dark. Choose Filter➥Fade➥Auto Levels. I set the Opacity at 70%.

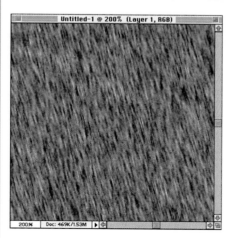

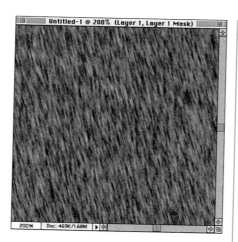

13 Create a layer mask. Select Image➥Apply Image (Source: Layer 1, Mode: Normal, Opacity: 100%). The layer mask uses the values in the layer to filter out some of the darker brown grass.

14 For further control over the color, you can select Image➥ Adjust➥Auto Levels. By changing the values in the layer mask, you make less of the layer visible. I used the Fade command (Filter➥Fade➥ Auto Levels) to set the Opacity of the Auto Levels adjustment to 34%, thereby undoing a large part of it.

15 Select Image➥Duplicate (Merged Layers only), or you could flatten the image. I prefer to duplicate the image—it allows me to keep the texture editable. The grass is okay the way it is, but it could be better. Choose Filter➥Sharpen➥ Unsharp Mask (Amount: 450, Radius: 1.5, Threshold: 0). The image becomes almost painfully sharp.

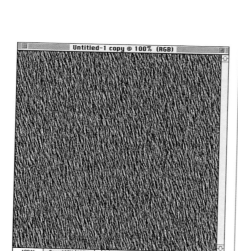

16 Select Filter➧Fade➧Unsharp Mask. I set the Opacity to 55%.

VARIATIONS

If you want to vary the colors in the grass, you can change the blending mode for Layer 1 to something other than Normal. The example shown here uses Hard Light mode, but Overlay, Multiply, Soft Light, Darken, and Luminosity modes also work well. The changes may be subtle.

To add a more drastic change to the color of the grass, change the Mode in Step 16 when you fade the Unsharp Mask filter. Almost every mode except Difference and Exclusion gives you a good result. Shown here is the grass with Darken mode selected in the Fade Unsharp Mask dialog box, and an Opacity of 100%.

To get this image, select Filter➧Fade➧Unsharp Mask and set the Opacity to 20%, and the Mode to Multiply.

To create a more stylized, decorative grass, in Step 15 select Filter➡Artistic➡Poster Edges. I used an Edge Thickness of 0, an Edge Intensity of 1, and a Posterization of 0.

Try making the grass texture seamless. After you have your finished texture, select Image➡Duplicate (Merged Layers only). Duplicate the Background layer. Select Filter➡Other➡Offset (Wrap Around). Make the Horizontal and Vertical distances one-half of the image dimensions. Create a layer mask. Use a soft 100-pixel paintbrush and black. Paint out the center area of the image in the layer mask leaving only the area around the rim. Try not to fog the tile. Select➡All. Define the pattern. Create a new file to the desired size. Fill with pattern.

Now, try making a grass that has a pebbly quality to it. After you have your finished texture, select Image➥Duplicate (Merged Layers only). Duplicate the Background layer. Turn off the Eye icon for the top layer and make the Background layer active. Select Filter➥Brush Strokes➥Ink Outlines (Stroke Length: 0, Dark Intensity: 20, Light Intensity: 10). Make the background layer copy active. Change the blending mode to Color Dodge and reduce the Opacity to around 46%. ■

Leather

You can make very convincing leather or cowhide easily using the Clouds, Noise, and Emboss filters.

1 Create a new file **640×480 pixels, RGB.** Change the foreground color to the color that you want to use for the duller leather accent color. I used RGB 185, 170, 150 (a dull beige). Change the background color to white.

2 Create a new layer. Select Filter➡ Render➡Clouds. Clouds is the only native Photoshop filter that works on a totally transparent layer. Reduce the layer opacity to 50%.

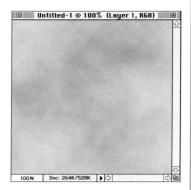

3 Change the foreground color to the color that you want to use for the brighter leather accent color. I used RGB 236, 144, 31 (a medium-strong orange). Change the background color to white.

4 Create a new layer. Apply Filter➡ Render➡Clouds. Change the blending mode to Multiply and reduce the layer opacity to 68%.

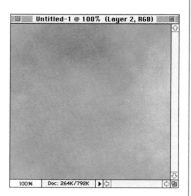

5 Make the Background layer active. Create a new layer. Double-click on the Layer name and change its name to "Texture layer." Fill with background color (white).

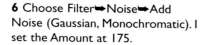

6 Choose Filter➡Noise➡Add Noise (Gaussian, Monochromatic). I set the Amount at 175.

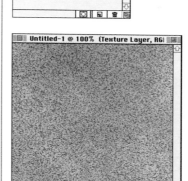

7 Select Filter➡Stylize➡Emboss. Typically, Angles of 37° or 137° look best. I used a 37° Angle, a Height of 3, and an Amount of 100%.

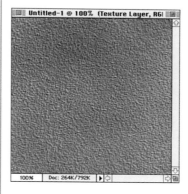

8 Select Filter➡Blur➡Gaussian Blur. The Amount of blur determines the smoothness of the leather. I used a Radius of 0.9.

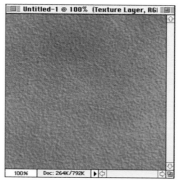

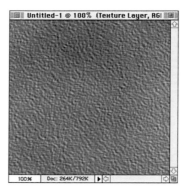

9 One could stop here, but I prefer a bit more pronounced texture. Choose Filter➡Stylize➡Emboss. Leave the Angle alone but vary the Amount or the Height. I used a Height of 4.

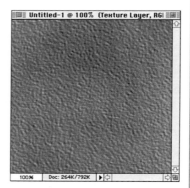

10 Choose Filter➡Blur➡Gaussian Blur. This time, I used a Radius of 0.5. You may continue the Emboss and Blur cycle until you are satisfied with the resulting leather.

VARIATIONS

You can vary the texture created by changing the type of noise used. Variations of the Grain filter (Filter ➡Texture➡Grain) work very well.

1 Complete the original example through Step 5. Choose Filter➡ Texture➡Grain. I used a Clumped Type with an Intensity of 49 and a Contrast of 26. Many other combinations are possible.

2 Choose the Threshold command (Image➡Adjust➡Threshold). I picked a Threshold Level about midpoint in the available range (186).

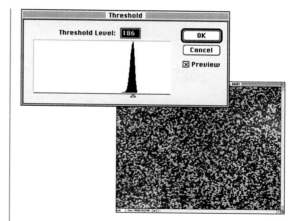

3 Choose Filter➡Blur➡Gaussian Blur. I used a Radius of 2.1.

4 Select Filter➡Stylize➡Emboss. I used an Angle of 37°, a Height of 3, and an Amount of 100%.

You can make a blistered leather by adding the Craquelure filter (Filter➡Texture➡Craquelure) after Step 8 of the original instructions. I used Crack Spacing of 19, Crack Depth of 5, and Crack Brightness of 7. I followed this with Filter➡ Stylize➡Emboss at an Angle of 37°, a Height of 3, and an Amount of 100%, and then applied a Gaussian Blur of 0.6.

You can make a truly pitted leather by applying the Craquelure filter a second time. I did not blur the filter afterward. ■

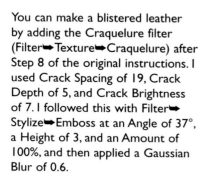

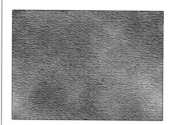

Goldgrad gradient
preset

You've heard the fairy tale about the girl the who spun straw into gold. This effect turns gold into linen (of course, you first have to create the gold).

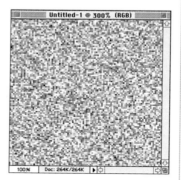

1 Create a new file. I used a tile size of 300×300 pixels. Choose Filter➡Noise➡Add Noise (Gaussian, do not check Monochromatic). I used an Amount of 135.

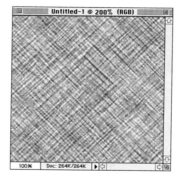

2 Select Filter➡Brush Strokes➡ Crosshatch. I used a Stroke Length of 21, Sharpness of 2, and Strength of 1. Choose Image➡Adjust➡Auto Levels to darken the effect.

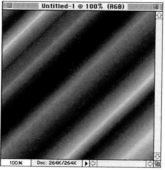

3 Create a new layer. Double-click the Gradient tool. Choose the Goldgrad gradient from the Gradients presets on the *Photoshop Textures Magic* CD-ROM. Use a Linear gradient. Drag the gradient from the upper-left corner to the lower-right corner of the image.

4 Choose Filter➤Distort➤Wave. The effect needs a Square Type. I used 23 Generators, Min. Wavelength of 4 and Max. Wavelength of 999, a Min. Amplitude of 23, and a Max. Amplitude of 174. I left the Horizontal and Vertical Scale at 100%, and set the Undefined Areas to Wrap Around.

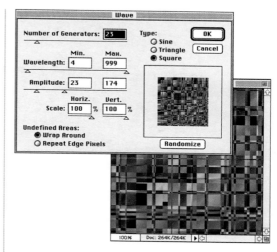

5 Choose Image➤Adjust➤ Hue/Saturation. Set the Saturation to +100. This causes only a small— but noticeable—difference.

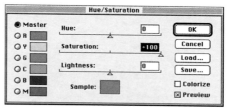

6 Change the blending mode to Color.

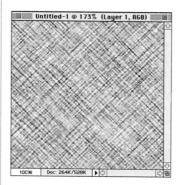

7 Duplicate Layer 1. Leave the Layer 1 copy at the top of the layer list. Make Layer 1 active. Change the blending mode to Hard Light.

8 Choose Filter➥Stylize➥Emboss (Angle: 37°, Height: 3). There is room to play with the Amount, however. I used an Amount of 167%. Because the layer is already in Hard Light mode, you can easily judge the effect that the Embossing filter creates.

9 Choose Image➥Duplicate. Check the Merged Layers Only box. You can certainly use the texture as it is now, if you like it, but it is just getting ready to become linen. Create the linen texture in the new, merged image.

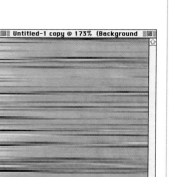

10 Duplicate the Background layer. Select Filter➥Blur➥Motion Blur (Angle: 0°). Set the Distance until you can barely see the vertical lines in the image. I used a Distance of 110.

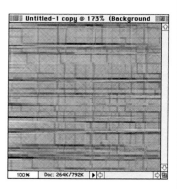

11 Reduce the layer's opacity so that you can see a bit of the original texture showing through. I set the opacity at 84%.

12 Duplicate the Background copy layer. Choose Layer➡Transform➡Rotate➡90° CW. Change the blending mode to Lighten. If you want a seamless pattern, make the pattern seamless using the Mosaic method. If you are going to print the texture, you should apply the Unsharp Mask filter (Filter➡Sharpen➡Unsharp Mask). I used a Radius of 1.4, an Amount of 140, and a Threshold of 0. The Threshold of 0 is reasonable because of this specific texture.

VARIATIONS

If you want a darker linen, you can add another step between Steps 7 and 8. Duplicate Layer 1. This creates Layer 1 copy 2, which is already in Hard Light blending mode. Apply the Emboss filter in Step 8 to this layer.

You can completely change the color of the linen if you want. After Step 12, create an adjustment layer. Make it a Hue/Saturation layer. I moved the Hue to −29, the Saturation to −59, and the Lightness to −26.

You can make an evenly woven fabric by using a large Distance on the Motion Blur in Step 10. I used a Distance of 590. I left the opacity at 100% by not completing Step 11. ▩

Marbled.Psd

Grape.Aco color
palette document

Many cultures throughout time have been fascinated by the design possibilities to be realized by dragging a stick through a bath of wet paint. Marbling has been practiced in Japan, China, Turkey, Persia, and throughout Europe. Today, marbled designs are being used in items as varied as book endpapers and children's sneakers. It is a much sought-after look. You can purchase stock photos of marbled papers for use on the computer, but you can also make some of your own. Here's a way to capture the beauty of marbling without the mess.

1 This effect uses the Photoshop Paths tool to create its magic. Open the file Marbled.Psd on the *Photoshop Textures Magic* CD-ROM. This file contains the paths that you need to get started.

2 Select your palette. You need three to six harmonious colors. I used the Grape.Aco Swatches document in the Swatches folder on the *Photoshop Textures Magic* CD-ROM. To place the color table into the Swatches palette, select Load Swatches from the Colors palette menu. The last five colors on the Swatches palette are the new ones.

3 Switch the foreground color to one of the new colors. I used the lightest green. Select Image➡ Duplicate to make a copy of the Marbled.Psd file. Fill the selection with foreground color.

4 Select the Paintbrush tool and the 100-pixel soft brush. Switch the foreground color to one of the other palette colors. Stamp circles of the color onto your image. Use all of the colors in your chosen palette in random or designed placement in the image. This acts as the base for the marbling process. I made a fairly regular distribution of the colors.

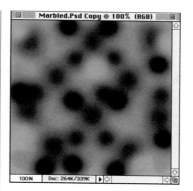

5 Double-click the Smudge tool. Set the Mode to Normal and the Pressure to 80%. Make sure that the Finger Painting box is *not* checked. Select the 21-pixel soft-edged brush (second from the right on row 2 of the default Brushes palette). Show the Paths palette. Click the path labeled Pass 1:T2B to make it active.

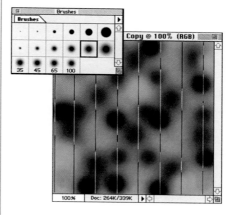

6 Click the second icon at the bottom of the Paths palette to stroke the path. Even though it says "Strokes path with foreground color," because you have the Smudge tool selected, the Paths will be smudged, not stroked. The Pressure of 80% causes the Smudge tool to pull the colors in the image along the path.

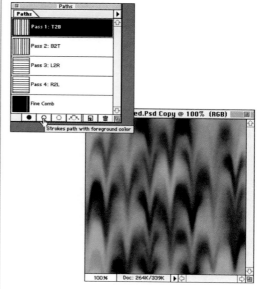

129

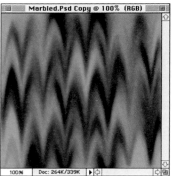

7 Change the Pressure setting on the Smudge Tools Options palette to 60%. Click the Pass 2: B2T path. Stroke the path as you did in Step 6.

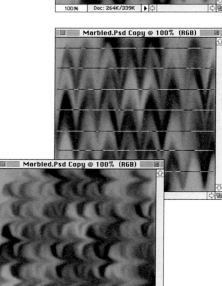

8 Click the Pass 3: L2R path. This path moves across the combed image from left to right. Stroke the path.

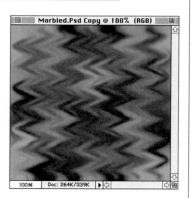

9 Click the Pass 4: R2L path. Stroke the path. This finishes the "traditional" combing process of the marble bath. Of course, you do not need to mix your colors this well if you prefer.

10 The last combing step gives the image its finished design. I chose to create a one-step "fine tooth comb" for this final path. Set the Pressure back to 80% in the Smudge Tools Options palette. Select a tiny brush (the 9-pixel brush that is second from the left on the second row of the default Brushes palette works well). Stroke the fine-tooth comb path.

VARIATIONS

Seamless Marble

If you want, you can easily make the marbled image seamless. This is a variation on the Center Cross method of creating a seamless pattern that is described in the "Photoshop Basics" section.

1 Use the finished marble tile. Duplicate the Background layer. Select Filter➡Other➡Offset (Wrap Around). Set the Horizontal and Vertical distances to one-half of the image dimensions. Create a layer mask. Use black, the Paintbrush tool, and the 100-pixel soft brush. Brush out the center seam line by painting over the area on the layer mask.

2 Create a new layer. (Option)[Alt] Merge Visible to a new layer. Select Filter➡Other➡Offset (Wrap Around). Create a layer mask. Use black, the Paintbrush tool, and the 100-pixel soft brush. Brush out the seam line near the edges by painting over the area on the layer mask.

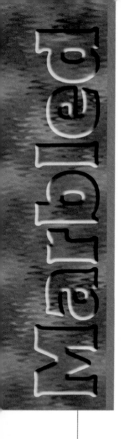

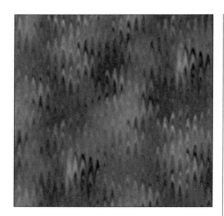

3 Create a new layer. (Option)[Alt] Merge Visible to a new layer. Select Filter➡Other➡Offset (Wrap Around). Check to make sure that your image is seamless. It should be. Touch-up using the layer mask if it is not.

Fancy Finish

You can use or create additional paths and finishing shapes. There are several more finishes in the Paths.Psd image on the *Photoshop Textures Magic* CD-ROM. The easiest way to create additional paths is to Select➡All. Choose Paths Palette menu➡Make Work Path. Copy this path and paste it into Adobe Illustrator. Fill the path in Illustrator and lock it. Draw the paths for the finished shape that you want. Duplicate it as many times as you need. Select all of the unlocked paths and copy them back into Photoshop. Paste as paths.

Complete Steps 1 through 7 of the original effect, using the colors of your choice. Open the Paths.Psd image. Drag the Wings2 path into your marbled image (make sure that no other path is selected at the same time). Click Wings2 to make it active. Stroke with the Smudge tool at 80% pressure and the 21-pixel soft brush. Make it seamless if you want. ■

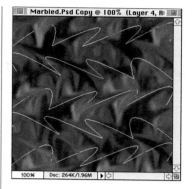

Metal

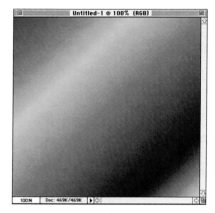

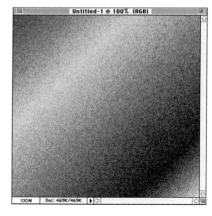

Brushed metal is an easy texture to create. If you manufacture enough, you can easily cover three-dimensional objects and various aliens with it.

1 Create a new file. I used one 400×400 pixels. Double-click the Gradient tool. Select the Golden preset that came from the *Photoshop Textures Magic* CD-ROM.

2 Drag the Gradient cursor from the top-left corner of the image to the bottom-right corner.

3 Apply Filter➡Noise➡Add Noise (Amount: 23, Gaussian, Monochromatic). You can fiddle with the Amount, but it needs to be low enough not to overwhelm the image.

4 Choose Filter➟Blur➟Motion Blur. I used an Angle of −47°, and a Distance of 37. These settings can be changed as you prefer.

5 Duplicate the Background layer. Change the blending mode to Lighten.

6 Apply Filter➟Blur➟Gaussian Blur. I used a Radius of 5. You will want to lighten the effect of the blurred noise on the metal, but it should still be visible.

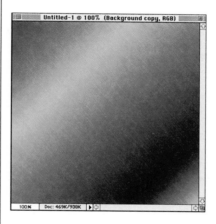

7 Create a new layer (Layer 1) by pressing the (Option)[Alt] key before you click the New Layer icon. In the dialog box, change the blending mode to Multiply and check Fill with Multiply—neutral color (white).

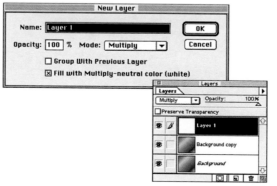

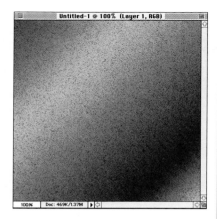

8 Apply Filter➡Noise➡Add Noise. Use a slightly higher Amount than before. This noise is on its own layer so that it can be manipulated separately, and so the opacity of the layer can be fine-tuned. I used an Amount of 45.

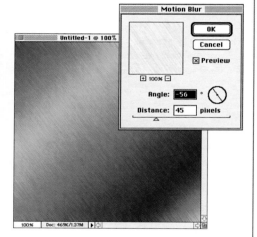

9 Choose Filter➡Blur➡Motion Blur. Use an Angle and a Distance that vary slightly from your first application of the filter. I used an Angle of −56° and a Distance of 45. Adjust the opacity of the layer if you want.

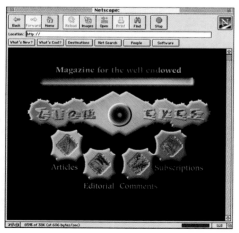

VARIATIONS

The same technique works on other precious metals as well. You can try the Copper Gradient preset...

...or the Silver Gradient preset from the *Photoshop Textures Magic* CD-ROM.

You could also use the Chrome preset, but it requires special handling. The Motion Blur in Step 4 needs to have a greater Distance to obliterate the color change line on the Chrome Gradient. I used an Angle of −62°, and a Distance of 640. In Step 8, I used a Noise amount of 110, and in Step 9, I used a Motion Blur angle of −47° (a decidedly different angle from the first blur) and a Distance of 640. These changes almost make the chrome surface look pitted. ■

137

If you have art in your soul, you have sometimes marveled at the colors in a piece of mother-of-pearl. Now you can create an electronic version. You could start with one of the "Opals" textures (page 146), or with a totally blank canvas. I'm going to show you how to begin from scratch.

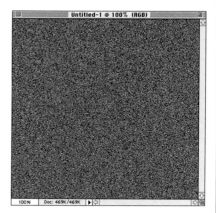

1 Create a new file. Mine is 400 × 400 pixels. Switch the foreground color to medium gray. I used RGB: 89, 89, 89. Fill with foreground color. Select Filter➡Noise➡Add Noise (Distribution: Gaussian, Monochromatic: Off). I used an Amount of 100.

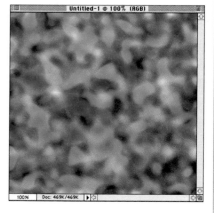

2 Choose Filter➡Blur➡Gaussian Blur (6.0). Select Image➡Adjust➡ Auto Levels. The color blobs should be bigger. Repeat the Gaussian Blur and Auto Levels to make the blobs the right size

138

TOOLBOX

Mother-Of-Pearl lighting effects preset

3 Duplicate the Background layer. Switch the foreground color to a darker gray. I used RGB: 69, 69, 69. Load the values of the layer (Command-Option-~)[Alt-Control-~]. Fill the selection with foreground color. Deselect. Change the blending mode to Multiply. When you load the values of the layer, you convert the values in the composite channel into a selection. The lighter values in the original accept more of the foreground color fill than do the darker values.

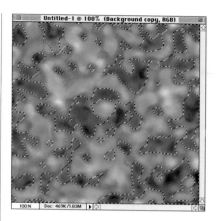

4 Create a new layer. (Layer 1) (Option)[Alt] Merge Visible to a new layer. Apply Filter➡Blur➡ Gaussian Blur (7.0). Change the blending mode to Darken.

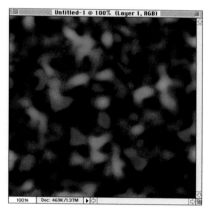

139

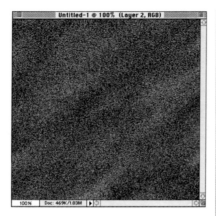

5 Create a new layer (Layer 2). (Option)[Alt] Merge Visible to a new layer. Select Filter➡Blur➡ Motion Blur. I used an Angle of 38°, and a Distance of 100 pixels. In this example, texture needs more lines. Select Filter➡Noise➡Add Noise (Distribution: Gaussian, Monochromatic: Off). I used an Amount of 100.

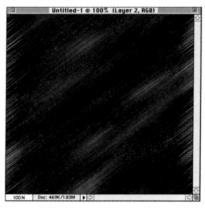

6 Choose Filter➡Blur➡Motion Blur. Reuse the last settings. The noise that you just added now helps to create the fine lines.

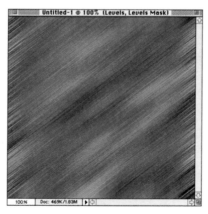

7 Create a Levels adjustment layer. Change the blending mode to Screen. Do not change the Levels histogram at all.

8 Duplicate the adjustment layer several times until the texture loses color (Screen mode makes the image lighter; with enough adjustment layers, you will end up with solid white). I created a total of three adjustment layers. I also set the layer opacity on the final adjustment layer to 80%.

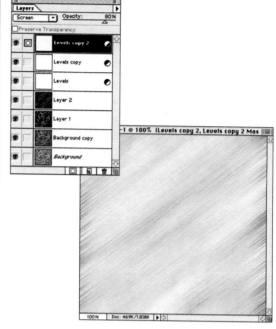

9 Make Layer 2 active. Apply Filter➡Blur➡Gaussian Blur. Apply just enough of a blur to smooth the rough lines from the image. I used a Radius of 2.8.

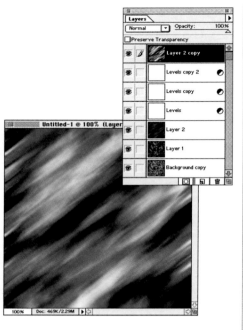

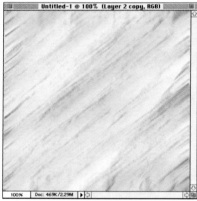

10 Mother-of-pearl is usually smooth, but not necessarily flat. You need to add texture and depth to your flat image. Duplicate Layer 2. Position the new layer at the top of the Layers palette list. Select Image➡Adjust➡Equalize and then Image➡Adjust➡Desaturate.

11 Select Filter➡Stylize➡Emboss (Angle: 29°, Height: 3, Amount: 100). This adds some streaky details. Change the blending mode of Layer 2 copy to Hard Light.

12 This step is optional. If you want to smooth out the texture a bit more, select Filter➡Blur➡Gaussian Blur. Apply just enough of a blur to smooth the rough lines from the image. I used a Radius of 2.8 again.

13 Create a new layer. (Option) [Alt] Merge Visible to a new layer. Choose Filter➡Render➡Lighting Effects. Use the settings shown, or select the mother-of-pearl preset from the *Photoshop Textures Magic* CD-ROM. You may want to search for the best channel to use for the texture channel. You want the lighting to be just a bit too bright, but if it's much too bright, turn down the Ambiance setting just a notch.

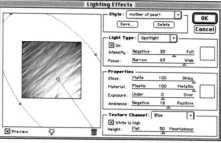

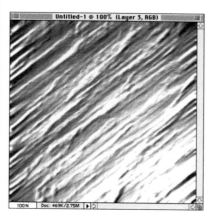

143

14 Select Filter➡Fade Lighting Effects. I set the opacity to 75%. Flatten the image.

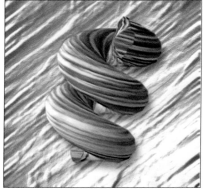

VARIATIONS

If you want a rougher texture, omit Step 9. Create a new channel (Channel 4). You can emphasize the fine lines by using the Apply Image command to copy Layer 2 to Channel 4. Make Channel 4 active. Select Image➡Adjust➡Auto Levels. Use Channel 4 in the Lighting Effects filter as the Texture channel instead of the Red channel.

If you want to start from the opal texture, apply Filter➡Blur➡Smart Blur (Threshold: 26, Radius: 21, Quality: High, Method: Normal). If you are using a high-contrast image, you can set both the Threshold and the Radius as high as they go. Select Filter➡Blur➡Motion Blur (Angle: 38°, Distance: 36). Create a new layer. Fill with white. Change the blending mode to Overlay. Create a new layer. Position the layer at the top of the layer list. (Option)[Alt] Merge Visible to the new layer. Change the blending mode to Screen. I set the layer opacity to 74%. ■

For as long as I can remember, I have been fascinated with the fiery color in the depths of the opal. The Opal effect will help you to re-create some of the fire of that most special of stones.

1 Create a new file. Mine is 400×400 pixels. Change the foreground color to neutral gray (RGB: 128, 128, 128). Fill with foreground color. Select Filter➡Noise➡Add Noise (Amount: 45, Gaussian, Monochromatic).

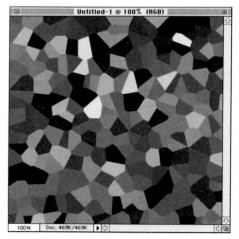

2 Choose Filter➡Pixellate➡Cyrstallize. I used a cell size of 38. The Gaussian Noise gives the Crystallize filter something to process. The result is a crystal network of gray shapes.

3 Select Image➥Adjust➥Auto Levels. Select Image➥Adjust➥ Posterize. Each level that remains in the image becomes a group of opal shapes. I left 5 levels. Decide upon the number of levels by watching the dialog box's preview. The different gray values in the image are reduced into fewer when you Posterize the image. Start by previewing 3 levels and look at the image at 4 to 8 levels as well. Pick the number that makes the most pleasing arrangement of gray values. Anywhere from 3 to 8 levels are manageable.

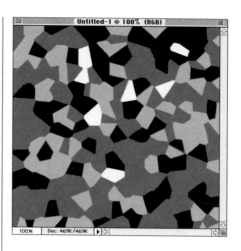

4 Double-click the Magic Wand tool. Set the Tolerance to 0, Anti-aliased on, and Sample Merged off. Click a white shape. Select➥ Similar. Change the foreground color to white (to match the color that you clicked). Create a new layer (Layer 1). Fill the selection with foreground color. Deselect. Turn on Preserve Transparency.

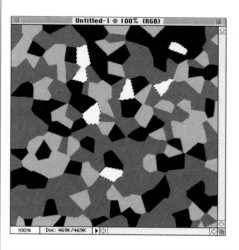

5 Choose Filter➥Noise➥Add Noise (Amount: 45, Distribution: Gaussian, Monochromatic: Off). If you choose Monochromatic noise, you will get no opal. Select Filter➥ Blur➥Gaussian Blur (4.0). Select Image➥Adjust➥Auto Levels. Opals begin to emerge. Steps 4 and 5 are the basic "create opal" steps. They are repeated (with some variations) for every level of gray that you selected when you posterized the image (which is why I suggest that you keep the number of levels fairly low).

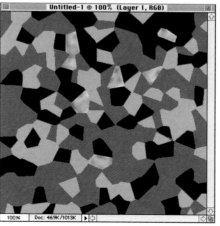

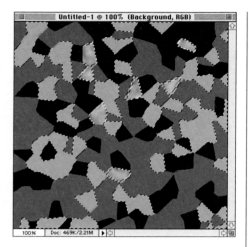

6 Make the Background layer active. Choose the Magic Wand tool and click the lightest gray in the Background. Select➡Similar. Choose the Eyedropper tool, and click inside the selected gray area to pick up a new foreground color. Create a new layer (Layer 2). Fill with foreground color. Deselect. Turn on Preserve Transparency.

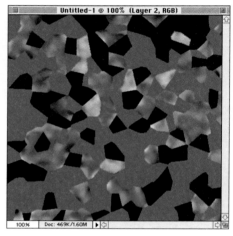

7 Choose Filter➡Noise➡Add Noise (Amount: 45, Distribution: Gaussian, Monochromatic: Off). Select Filter➡Blur➡Gaussian Blur (6.0). Next, select Image➡Adjust➡Auto Levels.

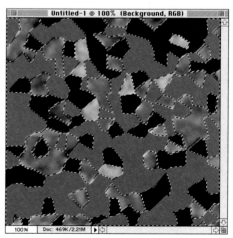

8 Make the Background layer active. Choose the Magic Wand tool and click another gray in the Background. Select➡Similar. Choose the Eyedropper tool, and click inside the selected gray area to pick up a new foreground color. Create a new layer (Layer 3). Fill the selection with foreground color. Deselect. Turn on Preserve Transparency.

9 Choose Filter➡Noise➡Add Noise (Amount: 90, Distribution: Gaussian, Monochromatic: Off). Select Filter➡Blur➡Gaussian Blur (5.0). Next, select Image➡Adjust➡ Auto Levels. The texture is more interesting if the opals are different in each layer. Choose Filter➡ Fade➡Auto Levels. Change the Opacity to 42%, and the Mode to Color Burn.

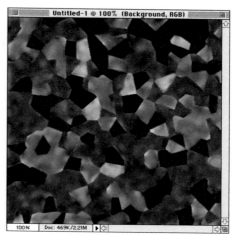

10 Make the Background layer active. Choose the Magic Wand tool, and click a black shape in the Background. Select➡Similar. Change the foreground color to black. Create a new layer (Layer 3). Fill the selection with foreground color. Deselect. Turn on Preserve Transparency.

11 Choose Filter➡Noise➡Add Noise (Amount: 45, Distribution: Gaussian, Monochromatic: Off). Select Filter➡Blur➡Gaussian Blur (2.0).Next, select Image➡Adjust➡ Auto Levels.

12 If there are any more gray levels, repeat Steps 6 and 7 until you have created opal layers for each color level in the Background layer.

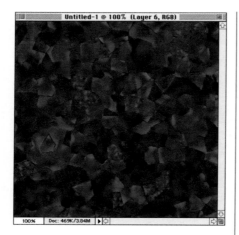

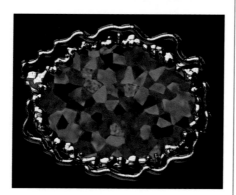

13 You could be finished…but maybe you'd like your opal to have a bit more drama. Make the Background layer the only visible layer by holding down the (Option) [Alt] key while clicking the eye icon in the Layers palette. Type (Command-Option-~)[Control-Alt-~]. This function loads the values in the Background layer as a selection. Change the foreground color to a medium-dark gray. I used RGB: 63, 63, 63. Turn on all of the layers again by holding down the (Option)[Alt] key and clicking the eye icon next to the Background layer in the Layers palette. Create a new layer. Position the layer at the top of the Layers palette list. Fill with foreground color. This places a range of gray shades over the other layers.

14 Now you can have fun with the layers. You might want to turn down the opacity of the top layer. I set it at 58%. I also changed the blending mode of Layer 5 to Hard Light, and reduce the layer opacity to 43%. This setting made the color stand out more.

VARIATIONS

If you change the blending mode on the top layer, you can create other interesting variations. Make the top layer active. Change the blending mode to Screen...

...or Overlay mode.

To change the texture from opal to abalone, select Image➡Duplicate (Merged Layers only). Change the foreground color to a shade of deep green. I used RGB: 73, 164, 65. Create a new layer. Fill with foreground color. Change the blending mode to Color Burn, and reduce the layer opacity to about 42%. Make the Background layer active. Apply Filter➡Pixellate➡Fragment several times. In my example, I used it three times. Finally, select Image➡Sharpen➡Unsharp Mask (Amount: 103%, Radius: 4.2, Threshold: 0). ■

Want to create miles of cracked, mistreated earth? Here's how. Create it to size, though, as this texture is not happy as a repeat.

1 Create a new file. Switch the foreground color to a deep brown or whatever earth color you prefer. I used RGB: 79, 58, 38. Fill the selection with foreground color.

2 Select Filter➠Noise➠Add Noise (Amount: 20, Distribution: Gaussian, Monochromatic). The Amount needs to be low enough so that you do not create white pixels. Use my settings first before you start experimenting with this one.

3 The parched earth effect is fairly easy to create, but it needs to be constructed in pieces. It will be easier to follow along if you name things the same way that I do—at least your first time through. Save the file as Parched.Psd (I'll just refer to it as "parched" for short).

4 Select Layers➠Duplicate Layer to place the Background layer into a new document that you should call "texture."

5 Choose Filter➞Other➞Minimum (2 pixels). This filter works on the darker pixels and is a way to increase the size of the noise.

6 Choose Image➞Adjust➞Auto Levels.

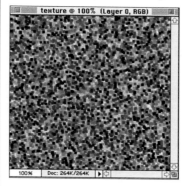

7 Select Filter➞Blur➞Gaussian Blur (1.5).

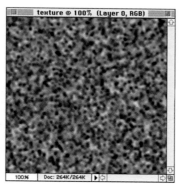

8 Let's emboss this without using the Emboss filter. Duplicate the Background layer (Background copy). Invert the copy (Command-I) [Control-I]. Reduce the layer opacity to 50%. The image turns a totally neutral gray.

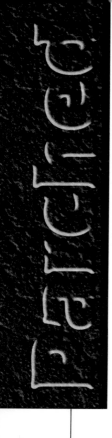

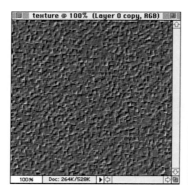

9 Press the (Command)[Control] key to access the Move tool, and use the arrow keys to move the top layer to the right and down several pixels. I moved the image two pixels right and two pixels down. This leaves a slight flaw at the left and top edges that you may want to trim off later.

10 Flatten the image. Drag and drop centered into the Parched image (Layer 1). Double-click on the name Layer 1 in the Layers palette, and change the layer name to Texture. Change the blending mode to Hard Light.

11 Make the Background layer active. Select Layer➡Duplicate Layer. Send the duplicate to a new image. Name the image Cracks.

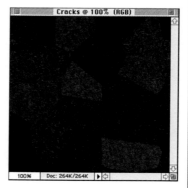

12 Select Filter➡Pixelate➡Crystal-ize. Choose a fairly large cell size. I used a cell size of 99. If you do not like the shapes that appear, select Undo, and reapply the filter. It will be slightly different at each applica-tion. We need to create two differ-ent images from this one.

13 Choose Filter➡Stylize➡Find Edges.

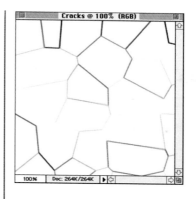

14 Select the Eraser tool and remove the lines that you do not like. Edit your "crack map" until it looks suitably cracked.

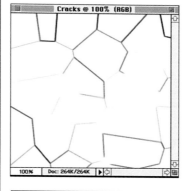

15 Drag and drop centered into the Parched image. It needs to be the layer above the Background layer (Layer 1). Double-click on the name Layer 1 in the Layers palette and name the layer Shadows. Change the blending mode to Multiply. The cracks are almost too light to see. Select Image➡Adjust➡Levels. Drag the left Input slider until the cracks become as dark as you want.

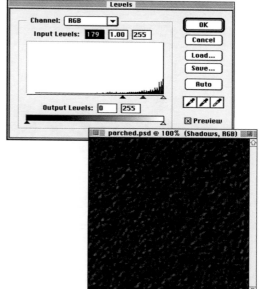

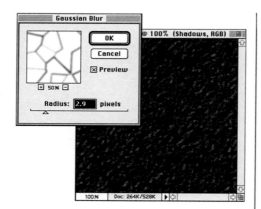

16 Apply Filter➡Blur➡Gaussian Blur (2.9) to soften the crack lines so that they begin to look like shadows.

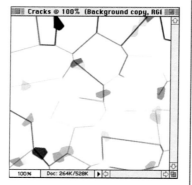

17 Now we need to create the crack embossing. Click on the Cracks image to make it active. Duplicate the Background layer. Change the blending mode to Multiply. Apply Filter➡Pixelate➡ Crystallize (Cell size: 24). The cracks that you generated originally with the Crystallize filter at size 99 aren't very natural. By adding more shapes on top of these, you can make a much more organic-looking set of cracks.

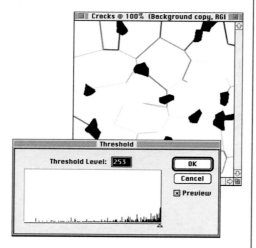

18 You need to make the new shapes black so that the final embossing works properly. Choose Image➡Adjust➡Threshold and move the slider to the right until all of the shapes turn black.

19 The shapes created are a bit too sparse. You really need to have most of the straight lines forming the original cracks covered with irregular shapes. Make the Background layer active. Duplicate the Background layer. Change the blending mode to Multiply. Apply Filter➡Pixelate➡Crystallize again with a new setting (Command-Option-F)[Alt-Control-F]. This time, use a cell size of about 17. The smaller shapes fill in quite nicely.

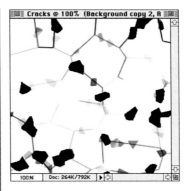

20 You also need to turn these shapes to black—or mostly black. This time, select Image➡Adjust➡Levels. Although you could use the Threshold command again, using Levels enables you to keep some of the shapes a lighter color. Drag the left Input slider almost all the way toward the right. As you can see, not all the shapes turn solid black this time.

21 You are almost ready to create the embossed crack map. You need to make the Background layer a bit darker so that some of the straight crack lines show up in the in the final embossing. Duplicate the Background layer (Background copy 3). Select Image➡Adjust➡Levels (Command-L)[Control-L]. Move the left Input slider until it is close to the right edge.

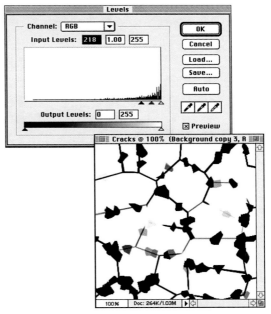

22 You now have a choice, and a decision to make. If you are *sure* that you like the cracks that have developed, you can flatten the image. If you want to give yourself the option to change your mind (without starting the example from scratch), (Option)[Alt] Merge Visible to a new layer. (That's what I usually prefer to do.)

> **TIP** You may be wondering why I didn't just leave the levels of the two crystallize layers and the Background layer alone and make them darker at this point—now that all three layers have been merged. You certainly can do that. You have more flexibility, however, doing it the other way (even if it is a bit more complex).

23 If you emboss the combined image now, you still get a jagged crack map. You need to blur the image before you emboss it to exaggerate its organic qualities and smooth out the rough edges. Select Filter➟Blur➟Gaussian Blur (2.3). But you're not done...

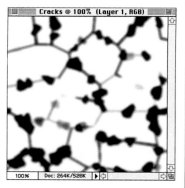

24 Select Image➨Adjust➨Levels
(Command-L)[Control-L]. You need
to move the left and right Input
sliders closer together. As you do,
the image will sharpen focus. If the
three sliders are more toward the
right, the image sharpens and fat-
tens. If the sliders are more toward
the left, the image still sharpens, but
the shapes get thinner. I prefer
something more centered but
toward the right as you can see in
the settings here. (One reason I
advocate the "keep the other layers" approach is that if you don't
like the embossing when you finally
get to do it, it is easy to (Option)
[Alt] Merge Visible the layers again
and try it again.)

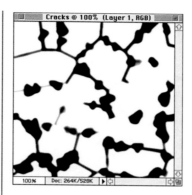

25 Finally…now you can apply
Filter➨Stylize➨Emboss (Height: 2,
Amount: 100%). I used an Angle of
−43° so that the cracks would sink
in to the ground and not come out
of it.

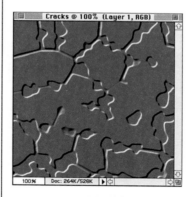

26 Drag and drop centered the
newly embossed layer into the
Parched image. Move the layer to
the top of the Layers palette.
Double-click on the layer name in
the Layers palette and change the
name to Embossed Cracks. Change
the blending mode to Hard Light.

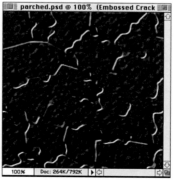

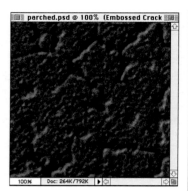

27 The image certainly looks interesting, but I've never seen ground with sharp white highlights! You need to tone down the Embossed Cracks layer. Select Filter➡Blur➡Gaussian Blur. A Radius of 2.3 is a good choice, although you could go higher or lower as you prefer.

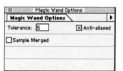

28 There is still a bit too much highlight to my taste. Parched earth shouldn't look like wet cobblestones. Change the blending mode to Normal so that you can see the layer as it actually is. Double-click the Magic Wand tool and set the Tolerance to 5, Anti-aliased on, and Sample Merged off.

29 Click one of the highlight edges and then choose Select➡Similar.

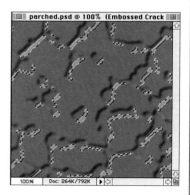

30 Change the blending mode to Hard Light. Hide the marching ants (Command-H)[Control-H]. Now you can see what happens as you select Image➡Adjust➡Levels (Command-L)[Control-L]. Drag the Gamma slider (the center slider) to the left edge of the values in the selection. Deselect.

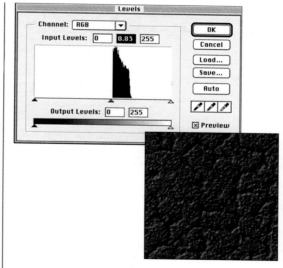

31 Select Image➡Canvas Size and reduce the dimensions by the amount of the "bad edges" from the hand embossing in Step 9. Anchor the image to the lower-right corner. I trimmed off two pixels on the top and left edge. Now all you need to do is to decide where to use your parched earth. ■

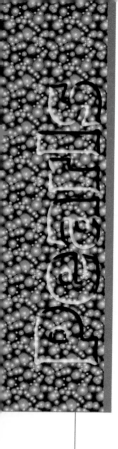

This technique creates small pearls that repeat seamlessly across an image. Variations can create effects that range from wild to caviar.

1 Create a new file. The file I used is 300×300 pixels. Switch to default colors.

2 Double-click the Gradient tool to bring up the Gradient Options. Set the Gradient to Foreground to Background, and the Type to Radial. Set the Apply mode to Darken, and the Opacity to 100%. Check Dither and Mask.

3 Turn on Rulers (Command-R) [Control-R]. Add a horizontal and vertical guide to the 150-pixel line along each ruler. The guides will cross in the exact center of the image.

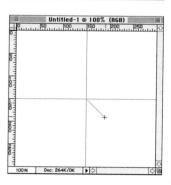

4 Place the cursor in the center of the image, drag it to the 180, 180 pixel marker to the bottom-right, and release. You will see one gradient circle.

5 Start the next circle a small distance away, and drag the rubber-band Gradient cursor so that it just overlaps the first circle. Release it. Because of the Darken mode, the circles seem to fuse where they touch.

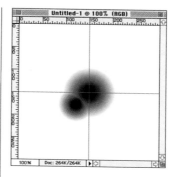

6 In order to make this pattern seamless, you need to place the circles carefully along the guidelines. Don't try to make them stay in a straight line—that looks awful when it is done. Fill in the image, only around the area that follows the lines. As you get near any of the sides, you need to make a circle that touches the side but does not get cut off by it. You may need to Undo your side circles a few times until you get them close enough without getting too close.

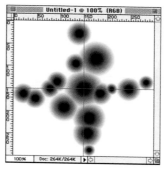

7 Choose Filter➡Other➡Offset (Right: 150, Down: 150, Wrap Around).

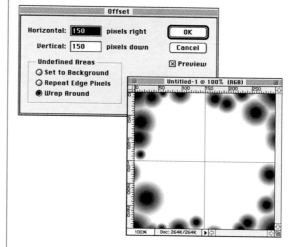

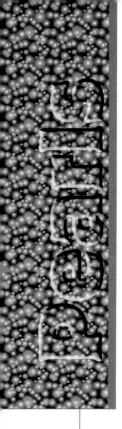

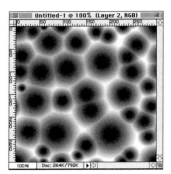

8 Now you have a tile that will definitely tile seamlessly, so you can fill in the rest of the image with more circles without having to worry about the way it wraps. Finish the image, but keep the size of the circles in synch with the sizes you have used so far.

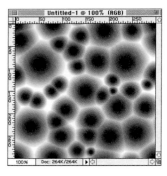

9 Reapply the Offset filter (Command-F)[Control-F]. Look carefully at the image. If you see any hard, sharp lines on the seam line, then cover them over gently with another circle. Make sure that your pattern is seamless.

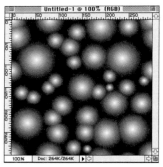

10 Invert the image (Command-I) [Control-I]. Wow! Pearls!

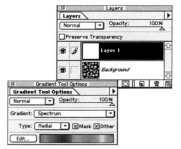

11 The next step is to add color. Create a new layer. Change the Gradient to Spectrum, and change the blending mode for the Gradient to Normal; however, keep it as a Radial gradient.

12 Turn on Rulers if they are off (Command-R)[Control-R]. Add a horizontal and vertical guide to the 250-pixel position on both rulers (there should already be guides at the 150-pixel center of the image. If you have removed them, re-create them, too). Place your cursor in the center of the image, and drag the rubber-band Gradient cursor to the intersection of the 250-pixel guide lines. Release the mouse.

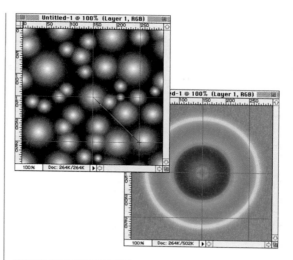

13 Change the blending mode to Color.

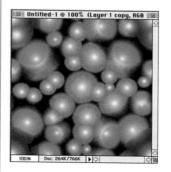

14 Duplicate Layer 1. The blending mode is already set to Color. Reapply the Offset filter (Command-F)[Control-F].

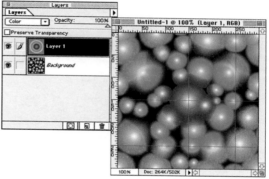

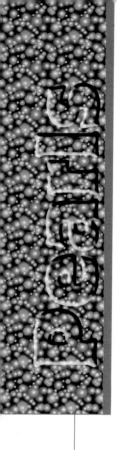

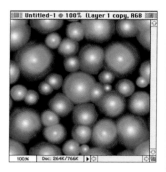

15 Reduce the layer opacity to 50%.

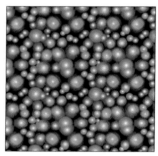

16 Select➥All. Define the pattern. Create a new file 1000×1000 pixels. Fill with pattern.

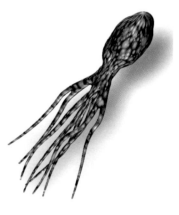

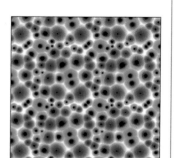

VARIATIONS

One thing you can do that is immediately interesting is to invert the image again. Now you have amoebas swimming in a test tube!

To create a festive image, click the pattern-filled image to make it active. Duplicate the Background layer. Rotate the top Layer 90° (Layer➡Transform➡Rotate 90° CW). Change the blending mode to Exclusion.

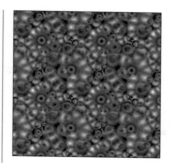

You can also try the following. Click the original pattern image to make it active. Choose Image➡ Duplicate➡OK, Merged Layers only. Duplicate the Background layer in this new image. Choose Layer➡Transform➡Rotate 90° CW. Change the blending mode to Difference. This makes a fractured texture with a black hole in the center (where the two layers were the same).

To fix the black hole, select Filter➡ Other➡Offset (Wrap Around). Play with the offset amounts until you no longer see the hole. I used 25 pixels right and 170 pixels down. The colors will change dramatically depending upon your offset amounts. Select all. Define a pattern. Create a new file 1000×1000 pixels. Fill the selection with pattern. ■

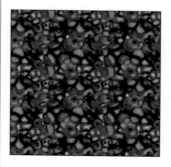

A riddle for you—"When is randomness not random?" The answer: when it is placed in repeat. Chaos theory is based on the order inherent at the heart of randomness—or is it the randomness at the heart of order? This effect takes you on a magic carpet ride through both kingdoms, and allows you to ponder the conundrum of order versus chaos at your own pace.

1 Create a new file. Because this is to be a tile, a small file works well. Mine is 50×50 pixels. Select Filter➡Noise➡Add Noise (Distribution: Gaussian, Monochromatic: Off). Use an Amount large enough to cover much of the white in the image. I used an Amount of 300. The tile is most definitely random.

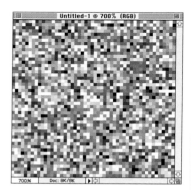

2 Create a new file that is twice the dimensions of the original tile. Mine is 100×100 pixels. Make the image seamless using the Mosaic method. This still looks random, but there is order emerging from the center of the tile along the seam lines.

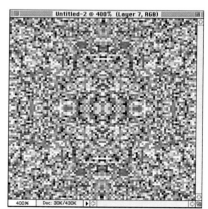

3 Select➡All. Define the pattern.
Create a new file. Mine is 430×680.
To make a magic carpet, you need a
file that is flying carpet-shaped. Fill
the selection with pattern. It's not
random now!

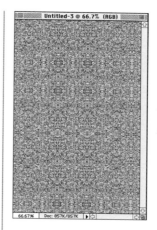

4 Choose two colors to be a border. Switch the foreground color to
your deeper color. Switch the background color to the brighter color.
I selected a royal blue and a bur-
gundy. Choose Image➡Canvas
Size. Increase the dimensions of the
file by the same amount in each
direction. Anchor in the center. I
added 50 pixels to both dimensions. The image is now bordered
by a 25-pixel swath of the brighter
background color on all four sides.

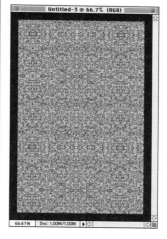

5 Switch foreground/background
colors. Choose Image➡Canvas
Size. Increase the dimensions of the
file by the same amount in each
direction. Anchor in the center. I
added 30 pixels to both dimensions. The image is now bordered
by a 15-pixel swath of the darker
background color on all four sides.

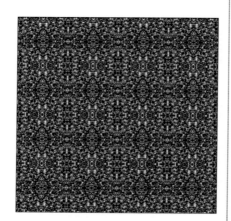

6 Double-click the Magic Wand tool. Set the Tolerance to 0 and Anti-aliased off. Click to select the inner border. Hold down the Shift key, and click to select the outer border. Fill the selection with pattern at 20–50% opacity. I used a 30% fill.

VARIATIONS

If you want a somewhat more practical use for this effect, it makes a wonderful bump or texture map. Complete Steps 1 and 2. Flatten the image. Convert the image to grayscale mode. Select Filter➡ Blur➡Gaussian Blur (.06). Select➡ All. Define the pattern. Create a new file of the desired size. Switch the foreground color to your desired pattern color. Fill the selection with foreground color. Create a new layer. Change the blending mode to Hard Light. Fill the selection with pattern.

To add an embossed texture to this, select Image➡Adjust➡ Threshold. Select a Threshold Value near the center. I chose a value of 128. Select Filter➡Blur➡Gaussian Blur. I used a Radius of 0.9 to just add back in a touch of gray. Choose Filter➡Stylize➡Emboss. I used an Angle of 120°, Height: 2 pixels, and Amount: 63.

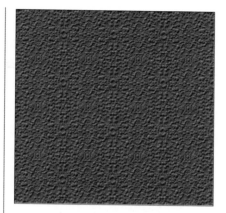

A softly blurred tile looks good too. Take the tile at the end of Step 2, select Image➡Duplicate (Merged Layers only). Select Filter➡Blur➡ Gaussian Blur (.09). Select➡All. Define the pattern. Create a new file of the desired size. Fill the selection with pattern.

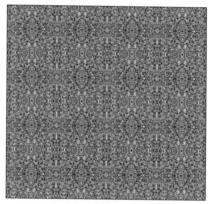

To get a slightly different look—one that is a bit glazed—create a new layer. Make the original unblurred image active. Select➡All. Define the pattern. Make the image with the new layer active. Fill with pattern. Change the blending mode to Darken. Apply Filter➡Blur➡ Gaussian Blur to the Background layer again if you want. The higher the blur, the more pronounced the glaze (until you blur the image so much that you can no longer distinguish any image at all). ■

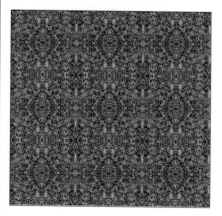

Japanese rice paper is truly a thing of beauty. Tiny flecks of color thread their way through the some-times lumpy texture of the paper. You can create an electronic ver-sion of rice paper and emboss and color it with no mess, and little fuss. Unlike real paper, it's immedi-ately dry and ready to go!

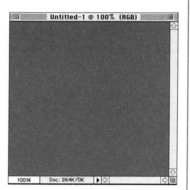

1 Create a new file. I used one 300×300 pixels. Switch the back-ground color to RGB: 98, 106, 191. Other colors can certainly be used, but you will get different results. Colors that are less saturated and medium-dark seem to work best—which is why I used a gray-blue as my starting color. Fill with back-ground color.

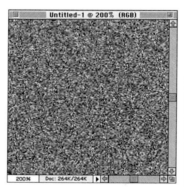

2 Select Filter➡Noise➡Add Noise (Distribution: Gaussian, Mono-chromatic Off). I used an Amount of 135.

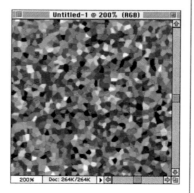

3 Choose Filter➡Pixelate➡ Pointillize. I chose a Cell Size of 6. Smaller sizes produce lighter and somewhat more delicate results. Much larger sizes become unusable for this effect. The background becomes the color between the "dots" created by the filter.

4 Select Filter➡Noise➡Median (3). This creates a watercolor-like base for the effect.

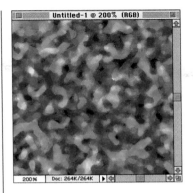

5 Duplicate the Background layer twice. Change the blending mode of the top layer to Darken.

6 If Background Copy 2 isn't the top layer, move it to the top of the Layers palette. Make the top layer invisible. Make the center layer (Background copy) active. Apply Filter➡Blur➡Motion Blur (Angle: 45°, Distance: 33 pixels). This streaks the image but does not obliterate it.

173

7 Make the top layer active. (It will become visible again as soon as you make it active.) Apply Filter➡Blur➡ Motion Blur (Angle: −45°, Distance: 33 pixels). This produces a criss-cross effect (because of the Darken mode), similar to the Crosshatch filter, but it's more controllable.

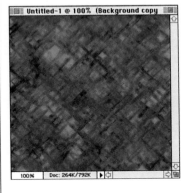

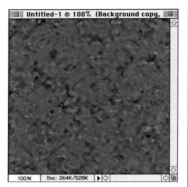

8 Select Layer➡Merge Down (Command-E)[Control-E]. Change the blending mode to Exclusion. The background areas of the image gray out, leaving threads of bright color. Here's why it's important to choose less saturated or medium-dark colors to start with—not all colors gray out this way in Exclusion mode.

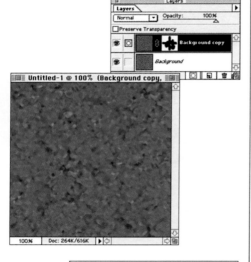

9 Flatten the image. Make the pattern seamless using the Masked Offset method.

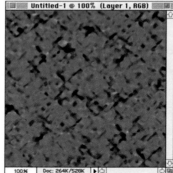

10 Flatten the image. Create a new layer. Select Image➡Apply Image (Channel: Green, Opacity: 100%, blending mode: Normal). Although you could use any of the color channels, the Green channel has the most consistently "good" (that is, clear and crisp rendering) image.

11 Change the blending mode to Hard Light. Choose Filter➡ Stylize➡Emboss. I used an Angle of −47°, a Height of 3 pixels, and an Amount of 100. The embossing gives a nice texture to the image.

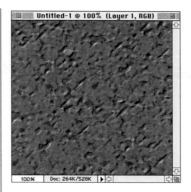

12 Select➡All. Define the pattern. Create a new file that is the desired size. Fill with pattern. I placed a layer of white over the pattern and then reduced the opacity to lighten the image.

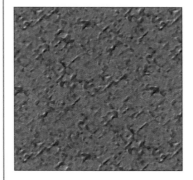

Dear Beth,
I am really enjoying my vacation. I miss you, though. I am anxious to get home and show you all of the pictures that I took.
Fondly,
Sister

VARIATIONS

If you want monotoned rice paper, work the original instructions through Step 11. Create a new layer. Switch the foreground color to your "stationery" color. Fill with foreground color. Change the blending mode to Color. ■

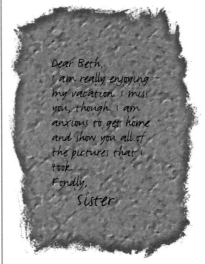

When I was young, my pockets were always filled with rocks. Their patterns and colors are endlessly fascinating. There are so many possibilities as you create this effect, that you may not want to stop! If you really want to model a specific type of rock, you can, but you can also create your own varieties.

1 Create a new file. This texture can be tiled, but real rock never repeats itself. I created a file 300×300 pixels. Switch the foreground color to your base "tone." I used RGB: 96, 121, 31—a grayed yellow-green. The color is not extremely critical as you can easily change it afterward. Fill the image with the foreground color.

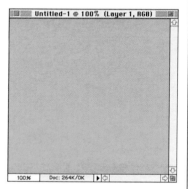

2 Create a new layer. Switch the foreground color to the second most used color in your palette. I used RGB: 255, 174, 111, which is a peach color. Fill the layer with foreground color.

3 Create a layer mask. This effect—which is similar in construction to Water—is actually built in the layer "mask." Switch to default colors (your colors should already be showing black and white when the layer mask is selected). Select Filter➡Texture➡Grain (Clumped). I used an Intensity of 40 and a Contrast of 50. Then apply Filter➡Noise➡Add Noise. I used an Amount of 65 to keep the noise from removing all traces of the Grain filter.

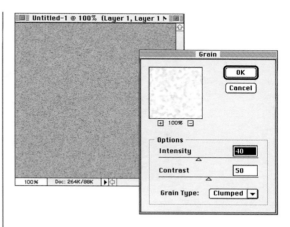

4 Select Filter➡Render➡Difference Clouds. Reapply this filter (Command-F)[Control-F] about 10 times to build up complexity.

5 You are still working in the Layer mask for this entire Step. Choose Filter➡Stylize➡Find Edges. The rock sample is supposed to be green with clumps of peach. If your image is too peach (and it almost certainly will be), select Image➡Adjust➡Invert (Command-I) [Control-I]. Then, select Image➡Adjust➡Auto Levels.

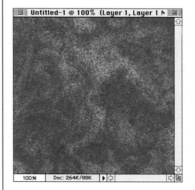

177

6 Create a new layer. Switch the foreground color to the third color in your palette. I used RGB: 56, 66, 31. Fill with foreground color. Create a layer mask.

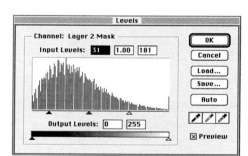

7 With the layer mask active, select Filter➡Render➡Clouds. Then apply Filter➡Render➡Difference Clouds—approximately 24 times (Command-F)[Control-F]. Choose Filter➡Stylize➡Find Edges. Select Image➡Adjust➡Auto Levels. The image will probably be mostly dark green. Select Image➡Adjust➡Invert (Command-I)[Control-I].

8 Choose Image➡Adjust➡Levels (Command-L)[Control-L]. Move the right and left Input sliders closer together as shown. This removes some of the layer mask detail and darkens what remains.

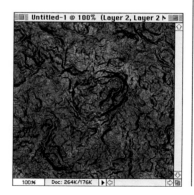

Levels dialog: Channel: Layer 2 Mask. Input Levels: 31, 1.00, 181. Output Levels: 0, 255.

178

9 Repeat Step 6 with a fourth color. I used RGB: 96, 0, 31—a strong wine tone. With the layer mask active, select Filter➡Render ➡Clouds. Then apply Filter➡Render ➡Difference Clouds once. Choose Filter➡Stylize➡Find Edges. The image will probably be mostly dark red. Select Image➡Adjust➡Invert (Command-I)[Control-I]. Select Image➡Adjust➡ Levels. Move the right Input slider to the start of the data. Move the left Input slider almost next to it as shown. The object is to leave only streaks of red in the image.

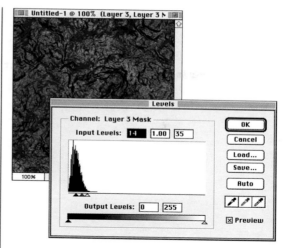

10 Duplicate Layer 1, which is the peach layer. Position the layer at the top of the Layers list. Make the layer mask active. Select Filter➡ Blur➡Gaussian Blur. I used a Radius of 2.0. You need a fairly small Radius for this to work well. Apply Filter➡ Stylize➡Find Edges. Select Image➡ Adjust➡Invert (Command-I) [Control-I]. Select Image➡Adjust➡ Auto Levels.

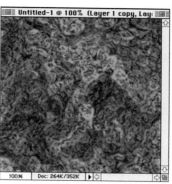

11 Select Image➡Adjust➡Levels. Drag the left Input slider part way toward the right to darken the peach streaks.

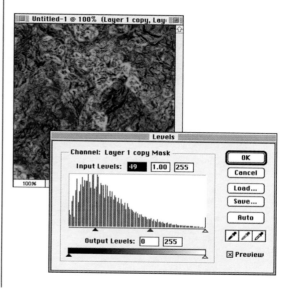

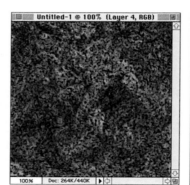

12 Repeat Step 6 with a fifth color. I selected RGB: 31, 46, 28—a very dark grayed-green. After you create the layer mask, switch foreground/background colors so that black is your background color. With the layer mask active, select Filter➡Pixelate➡Pointillize (5). Apply Filter➡Stylize➡Find Edges two times.

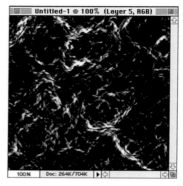

13 Create a new layer. Select Image➡Apply Image. Make Layer 3 the source Layer and the Layer Mask the Channel.

14 Change the blending mode to Hard Light. Choose Filter➡Stylize➡Emboss (Angle: 132°, Height: 2 pixels, Amount: 77).

15 Temporarily change the blending mode to Normal. Load the selection from Layer 5 (Command-Option-~) [Control-Alt-~]. Select Image➡Adjust➡Levels (Command-L) [Control-L]. Move the white Output slider to about 225 to cut down on some of the embossed highlights. Change the blending mode back to Hard Light.

16 Create a new layer. Switch to default colors. Select Filter➡Render➡Clouds. Then select Filter➡Noise➡Add Noise (Distribution: Gaussian, Monochromatic). I used an Amount of 65. Choose Filter➡Sketch➡Plaster (Image Balance: 20, Smoothness: 2. Light Position: Top). This makes another rough surface. Apply Image➡Adjust➡Threshold and leave the balance near the center. Change the blending mode to Hard Light. Choose Filter➡Stylize➡Emboss (Angle: 130°, Height: 2 pixels, Amount: 100). Select Filter➡Blur➡Gaussian Blur (0.6) to smooth the embossing a little bit. ■

The Displace filter can be used in conjunction with the Darken blending mode to create interlaced patterns of seemingly great complexity. Here I use it to create a metallic rosette pattern.

1 Create a new file 300×300 pixels. Turn on the rulers (Command-R) [Control-R]. Add a horizontal guide at the 150-pixel mark. Add a vertical guide at the 150-pixel mark.

2 Double-click the Gradient tool. Use the Copper2 preset from the *Photoshop Textures Magic* CD-ROM and change the Gradient Type to Radial.

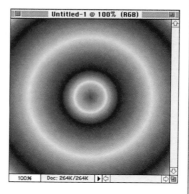

3 Place your cursor in the center of the image and drag it to the upper-right corner to create a radial Gradient. Hide the guides (Command-;)[Control-;] and turn off the rulers (Command-R) [Control-R].

4 We need to create a displacement map—an image that the Displace filter uses to move the pixels in the image being filtered. Black and white pixels in the displacement map create the most movement. Create a new file 300×300 pixels, grayscale mode. Select the rectangular Marquee tool and set a fixed size to 300 pixels wide × 50 pixels high. Drag the marquee to the top of the image. Switch to default colors. Fill with foreground color.

5 Set the fixed size of the rectangular Marquee to 300 pixels wide × 100 pixels high. Drag the marquee to the top of the image (it will select 50 black and 50 white pixels).

6 Select→All. Define the pattern. Deselect. Choose Filter→Blur→ Gaussian Blur (1.0). Save the file as Displace.Psd.

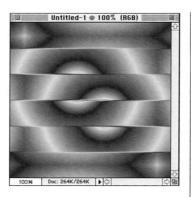

7 Click on the gradient image to make it active. Choose Filter➡ Distort➡Displace. I made the Horizontal and Vertical Scales both 20%, and set the Displacement Map to Stretch to Fit and the Undefined Areas to Wrap Around. Click OK. When you are prompted for the name of the file to use as a displacement map, select the Displace.Psd that you just created.

8 Duplicate the Background layer (Background copy). Select Layer➡ Transform➡Rotate 90° Clockwise.

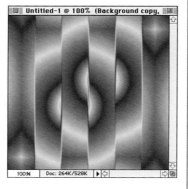

9 Change the blending mode to Darken. This is the basic pattern unit, but it needs to be made seamless before you use it.

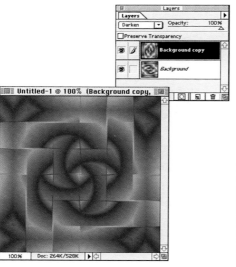

10 Make the pattern seamless using the Mosaic method.

VARIATIONS

If you want an even stronger rosette in the center of the pattern, after you have displaced the image in Step 7, apply Filter➡Distort➡ Displace again using a Scale factor of −10%, both horizontally and vertically. Set the Displacement Map to Stretch to Fit and the Undefined Areas to Wrap Around. Use the Displace.Psd map that you created. Make the pattern seamless using the simple method.

To create a pattern that does not have a strong center, you can use the Copper gradient preset that comes with Photoshop 4.0. Follow all of the original instructions, but choose the Copper gradient instead of the one provided on the *Photoshop Textures Magic* CD-ROM.

You can get an interlaced effect with a little bit more work. I used the Copper gradient as the starting point because that enhances the interlaced effect. Complete the original instructions through Step 7 (except for the choice of the gradient). Duplicate the Background layer. Use the Numeric Transform command (Shift-Command-T)[Shift-Control-T] to rotate the layer 60°. Duplicate the background layer again. Use the Numeric Transform command again to rotate the layer −60°. Make the Background copy layer active. Change the blending mode to Darken. Define the pattern. Fill any desired selection with the pattern.

Finally, you can get a hexagonal interlaced effect. Use the same instructions as used in the interlaced effect. When you duplicate the Background layer a second time, use the Numeric Transform command (Shift-Command-T) [Shift-Control-T] to rotate the layer 120°.

You can use this hexagonal effect (or any of the others) as a bump map rather than as a pattern. Create a new file of the desired size. Switch the foreground color to the color that you want your texture to be. I chose RGB: 154, 161, 204. Fill with foreground color. Create a new layer. Fill with one of the pattern variations. Select Image➥Adjust➥Desaturate (Shift-Command-U)[Shift-Control-U]. Choose Filter➥Stylize➥Emboss (Angle: 147°, Height: 3 pixels, Amount: 100). Change the blending mode to Hard Light. ■

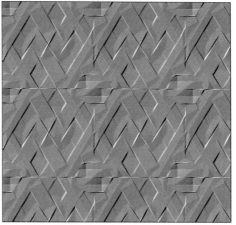

I have always lived about an hour away from the New Jersey shore, and my summers growing up were spent, in part, by the sea (or "down the shore" as the Philadelphiaism goes). I remember spending hours drawing in the wet sand as the tide receded. I used my finger, a convenient seashell, or a left-over popsicle stick from the Good Humor man. This texture pays fond tribute to those idyllic long-gone days.

1 Open the file 03N31.eps from the *Photoshop Textures Magic* CD-ROM. Because it is a vector file, you are asked to select a size for it within Photoshop. Set the width to 100 pixels, constrain the proportions, and check the Anti-aliased box.

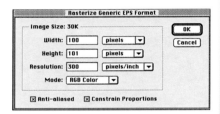

2 Select Image➡Canvas Size and change the size to 300×300 pixels. Leave the Anchor in the center. This gives your pattern more room and centers it all at the same time. Create a new Background layer.

3 Duplicate Layer 1. Choose Layer➡Transform➡Flip Horizontal. This adds variety to the pattern-to-be. Select Filter➡Other➡Offset (Wrap Around). Make the Horizontal and Vertical distances one-half of the image dimensions (in this case, 150 pixels right and 150 pixels down).

4 Open the file 01K29.eps. Rasterize it at 100 pixels wide, Constrain Proportions, and select Anti-aliased. Drag and drop centered into the pattern file. Choose Layer→ Free Transform (Command-T) [Control-T]. Place the cursor outside of the bounding box and rotate the crab slightly. (The figure shown here has the lower two image layers made invisible for clarity). Press (Enter)[Return] to execute the transformation.

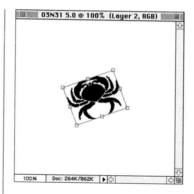

5 Select Filter→Other→Offset (Wrap Around). Make the Horizontal distance one-half of the image dimensions (150) and the Vertical distance 0.

6 Duplicate Layer 2. Reapply the Offset filter (Command-F) [Control-F]. This puts the new layer back into the center. Select Layer→ Transform→Flip Horizontal. Select Filter→Other→Offset (Wrap Around). Make the Horizontal distance 0 this time, and the Vertical distance one-half of the image dimensions (150 pixels). This sends the crab to the top and bottom of the image.

189

7 You now have a completely seamless pattern, but there is still a lot of white space. Open the files 03N31.eps (Hand), 06A11.eps (Arrow), 08B33.eps (Heart), and 07D04.eps (Spiral). Rasterize these at 50 pixels wide, Constrain Proportions, Anti-aliased on.

8 Drag and drop the star into the white space on the upper-left. Do not try to center it in the space—the result is more interesting if you preserve some randomness. Drag and drop the spiral into the upper-right white space, the heart into the lower-left, and the arrow into the lower-right. If you want, rotate the arrow slightly so that it does not seem so artificial.

9 Select➤All. Define the pattern. Create a new file that is three times the tile size (900×900 pixels). Fill with pattern. You need to work the remaining steps inside of a repeated pattern so that you have a 300 pixel square seamless repeat at the end. The Find Edges filter and the Emboss filter that you will use leave artifacts along the image edges. If you were to continue working in the 300-pixel tile, your final tile would not be seamless.

10 Choose Filter➤Stylize➤Find Edges. This looks nice just as it is (and could make a good background for an ad)!

11 Choose Filter➥Stylize➥Emboss (Angle: 151°, Height: 2 pixels, Amount: 100). When you finish all of the embossing to be done (a total of three times), the lines will look as if they are drawn in the sand. For this to work, you need to raise the embossing, not sink it into the texture—so keep the angle positive.

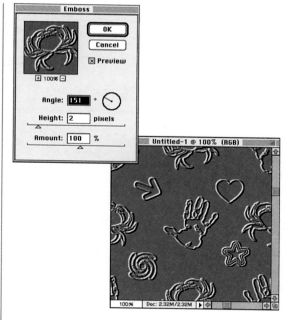

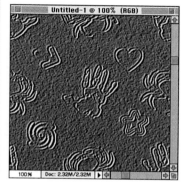

12 Emboss the image again (Command-F)[Control-F].

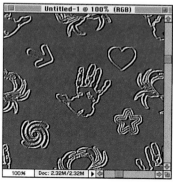

191

13 Select Filter➥Noise➥Add Noise (Distribution: Gaussian, Monochromatic). I used an Amount of 42. You don't want the noise to overwhelm the image. Select Filter➥Blur➥Gaussian Blur (0.5). Use a very small blur here. Choose Filter➥Stylize➥Emboss (Angle: 151°, Height: 2 pixels, Amount: 100). Reuse the settings from the previous steps. Your artwork is now etched in sand.

14 Gray sand is not particularly appealing. Create an adjustment layer for Hue/Saturation. Click Colorize. I moved the Hue to 50, the Saturation to 20 and the Lightness to +8. You can pick your favorite "sand" color.

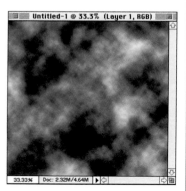

15 The sand in tidal areas is not flat. In addition to the sand texture, you can see where the waves lapped against the beach and then receded. You can simulate that play of waves. Create a new layer at the top of the Layers list. Switch to default colors. Choose Filter➡ Render➡Clouds.

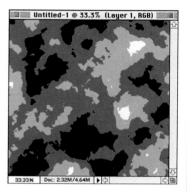

16 Select Image➡Adjust➡ Posterize. I used 5 levels, but this depends on the clouds formation in your image. Pick a number of levels that looks good to you, but keep it relatively simple.

17 Select Filter➞Noise➞Add Noise (Distribution: Gaussian, Monochromatic). I used an Amount of 42. Select Filter➞Blur➞Gaussian Blur. Use the same settings as before (0.5). Emboss the image with the same settings used in Step 11. Change the blending mode to Hard Light. You now have an instant trip to the shore.

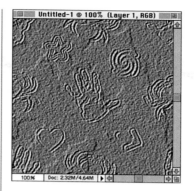

18 Select the rectangular Marquee and set a fixed size to 300×300 pixels (or the size of your original tile). Drag the Marquee into the center of the image. It need not be exactly the center, but it needs to be near the center. Define the pattern. Create a new file of the desired size for your intended use. Fill with pattern. Once you are sure that your repeat is seamless, you can crop (Image➞Crop) the 900×900 pixels image down to the single repeat tile.

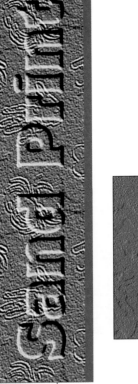

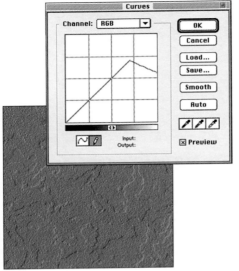

VARIATIONS

If you want just the sand texture and no pattern, start your image from Step 15. When you have constructed the sand, Create an adjustment layer for Hue/Saturation above the sand. You can make a repeat pattern from sand, but it is more natural if you create it at the needed size. If the highlights are too strong from the embossing, choose Image➡Adjust➡Curves, and use the Pencil tool in the Curves dialog box as shown to cut off some of the highlights.

Slate

To create slate, create a new file at the final size for your texture (slate doesn't repeat well either). Change the foreground color to a deep charcoal gray. Fill the image with the foreground color. Select Filter➡Noise➡Add Noise (Distribution: Gaussian, Monochromatic Off). I used an Amount of 56. Choose Filter➡Pixelate➡Crystallize. I used a cell size of 24 but almost any amount is okay. Select Filter➡Fade Crystallize. Change the blending mode to Multiply and reduce the opacity to 50%. Select Filter➡Blur➡Motion Blur (Angle: 0° or something near to that). Set the distance to something that does not destroy the range of colors. I used 120. Select Image➡Adjust➡Desaturate. Then select Filter➡Fade Desaturate. Change the blending mode to Dissolve and reduce the Opacity to 50%. Create a new

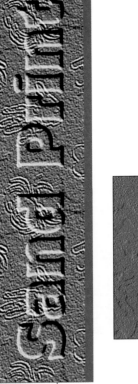
Sand Print

layer. In this layer, complete Steps 15 and 16 from the original instructions. Double-click the rectangular Marquee tool. Make sure the Feather is set to 0 and the Style is Normal. Select the left 1/5 of the image (across the full height of the image, but only about 1/5 of the width). You need to stretch the posterized clouds to elongate them in a manner similar to slate. Choose Layer➡Free Transform (Command-T)[Control-T]. Drag the middle handle on the right side of the selection until it reaches the right side of the image. Press (Enter)[Return] to execute the transformation. Proceed with Step 17. For added highlights, duplicate Layer 1.

You can also use only the offset technique from Steps 1 through 9 to create a comic-book like wrapping paper effect. If you use a single application of the Emboss filter and a subdued setting on the Hue/Saturation layer, you create a well-bred wrapping paper...

...or, you can use all primary colors and apply Filter➡Pixelate➡Color Halftone to the clip art, and create a very wild wrapping paper. Both of these images use the animals from the Art Parts clip art collection from FontHaus. ▪

Picture waves breaking at the shore, and the sea foam boiling as the tide crashes up against dry land. This effect will never win a photographic look-alike competition, but it is a good artistic substitute. Besides, you never know when you might want to draw a fish tank. Sea foam can also be sized correctly for printing—it looks even more realistic when viewed at lower than 1:1 ratio on your screen.

1 Create a new file. Mine is 600×400 pixels. This version is not seamless, so make the file as large as you want your texture to be. Switch the foreground color to a medium sea green. I used RGB: 16, 141, 119. Switch the background color to a deep sea green/blue. I used RGB: 39, 71, 61.

2 Double-click the Gradient tool and change the Gradient to Foreground to Background, set the opacity to 100%, and set the Type to linear. Drag the Gradient cursor from the top-left corner of the image to the bottom-right.

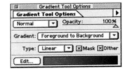

3 Change the opacity of the Gradient tool to 30%. Place the Gradient cursor in the center of the image and drag on a straight line to the bottom of the image. This adds another subtle dimension to the Gradient.

4 Switch the background color to a dark navy blue. I used RGB: 0, 42, 99. Set the Gradient opacity to 10%. Create a new layer. Drag the Gradient cursor from the top to the bottom of the new layer. Add two additional gradients to this layer. Both should move on the diagonal. Place one from top-left to bottom-right, and the other from top-right to bottom-left. Let both of these gradients start and end about 1/4 of the distance from the edge of the image.

5 Create a new layer. Switch the foreground color to a greener sea green. I used RGB: 0,124.94. Switch the background color to a gold or rust. I used RGB: 130, 100, 23.

6 Change the Gradient tool opacity to 60%. Drag the Gradient cursor from about 1/8 of the way from the top to about 1/8 of the distance from the bottom. These three layers are your background "sea." If you are not happy with the color, you can adjust it now, or do it later (because there is no pressing need to flatten the layers).

7 Create a new layer. Switch to default colors. Fill the layer with the background color. Select Filter➡ Pixelate➡Pointillize. I used a cell size of 9, though you might want a smaller one if you are going to use this texture at 72 dpi. The Pointillize filter uses your background color as the background behind the dots that it creates. For this effect to work, the background color selected in the toolbox must be white.

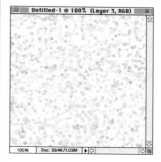

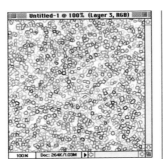

8 Select Filter➡Stylize➡Find Edges. Choose Image➡Adjust➡Auto Levels to make the edge colors sharper.

9 Here's where it gets tricky. Show the Channels palette. Load the selection in the Composite channel by (Command)[Control]-clicking the RGB channel name in the Channels palette. This creates a selection from the values in the RGB channel. Pixels that are white are totally selected; darker pixels are proportionally less selected. Press the Delete key. *Do not deselect.*

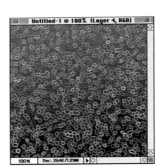

10 At this point, you have a wonderful background for water in a fish tank. Create a new layer. Reverse the selection (Select➡ Inverse). Fill with your background color (white). *Do not deselect.*

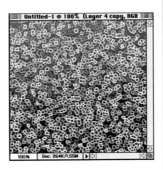

11 Duplicate Layer 4 (Layer 4 copy). Fill with the background color (white). You may need to fill this layer several times—because the selection is partially transparent, it will become whiter each time you fill it.

12 Duplicate Layer 4 copy. Select Layer➥Transform➥Flip Horizontal. Deselect. This just mixes the foam up a bit more.

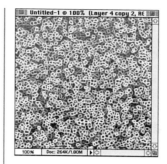

VARIATIONS

If you want to make the foam look like it is cresting a wave, choose Image➥Rotate Canvas➥90° CW after you have finished the texture. (You really *do* want to rotate the image rather than the layer.) Now, apply Filter➥Distort➥Shear. You rotated the canvas just to apply this filter. Drag the center point of the line to the second line to the left on the graph as you see in the settings here. Click OK. Select Image➥ Rotate Canvas➥90°CCW, which puts the image back into its original orientation. Now it looks as if the wave is just breaking. ■

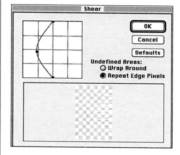

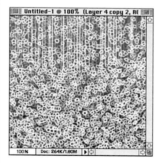

Snakes are not usually the most favorite things to contemplate. Most folks find reptiles to be so…reptilian! But snakeskin is a prized fabric, and the range of patterns possible on snakes is breathtaking. In this simulation, you will generate an organic (that is, random but naturalistic) shape for the snakeskin pattern. It may not resemble a real breed, but it will be both individual and unique—your own species of snake—as flamboyant or subtle as you prefer.

1 Create a new file. Mine is 300×300 pixels. In this file, you will create the basic snakeskin repeat. The scales will come later. Switch to default colors. Select Filter➡Noise➡Add Noise (Distribution: Gaussian, Monochromatic Off). I used an Amount of 135.

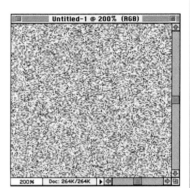

2 Apply Filter➡Pixelate➡Pointillize. I used a cell size of 35, but the size is not really critical.

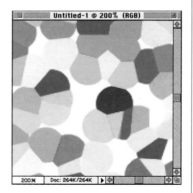

3 Select Filter➡Blur➡Gaussian Blur (60). It is important that a very large blur be used in order to generate a few possible lines that become the snakeskin pattern. Choose Image➡Adjust➡Auto Levels.

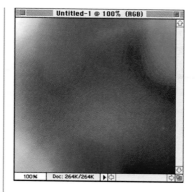

4 Select Filter➡Stylize➡Trace Contour. I used a Level of 101 with an Upper Edge. When you apply this filter, you see curved, organic lines. Choose the setting that gives you an interesting line or shape in any of the three colors that it shows. Later the shapes will be filled with a series of radial gradients to create the snakeskin background, so it is important that you like the curves.

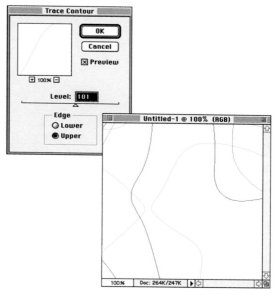

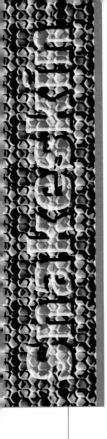

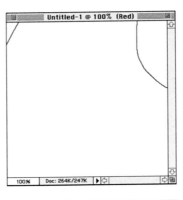

5 Make the Channels palette active. Make each channel active, one by one, to see which one has the most interesting shape. I like the Blue channel best.

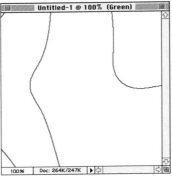

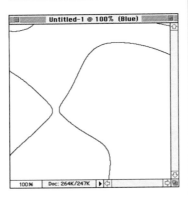

6 Duplicate the channel to a new document (Untitled-2). Convert the image to Grayscale mode. Convert the image to RGB mode. (You cannot go directly from Multichannel—the image mode that was duplicated—to RGB.)

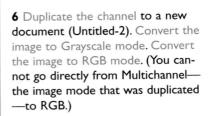

7 Double-click the Magic Wand tool and set the Tolerance to 10 with Anti-aliased on. Click inside of one of the shapes to select it. Choose Select➡Modify➡Expand (1 pixel). This allows you to cover the line.

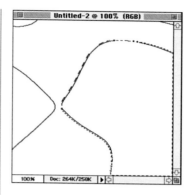

8 Switch the foreground color to the starting color for one gradient. Switch the background color to the ending color for the gradient. I used red and black. Double-click the Gradient tool and select a Fore-ground to Background radial gradi-ent (or build your own, more com-plex one if you prefer). The center of the gradient leaves an "eye," so you need to determine where you want it to be. Place the cursor at the desired center location in the selection and drag to create the gradient.

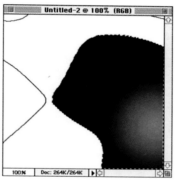

9 Select and color any additional areas in which you want to use the same gradient.

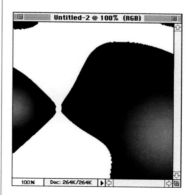

203

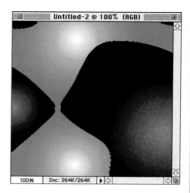

10 Select one or more areas with a new set of gradient colors. I chose a green-to-white gradient.

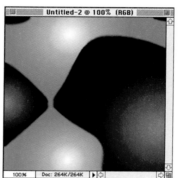

11 Smooth out any rough areas between the gradients using the Blur tool at 100% pressure.

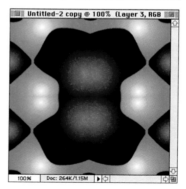

12 You now have the base repeat unit for the snakeskin. The pattern, however, is probably too large. Save it for future reference. Select Image➡Duplicate. Choose Image➡ Image Size and reduce the image to 50%.

13 Create Layer 0. Select Image➡ Canvas Size. Anchor the image to the top-left corner and double the image dimensions. Make the pattern seamless using the Mosaic method. Select Layer➡Merge Visible. You will still have a layer (the image should not be flattened).

14 Select Image➡Image Size and reduce the pattern to your desired width. I set a size of 100×100 pixels to give me a tile that is 1/3 inch in print. Choose Image➡Canvas Size, double the height, and anchor the image in the top center.

15 Duplicate the layer. Select Filter➡Other➡Offset (Wrap Around). Make the Horizontal and Vertical distances one-half of the image dimensions. Select Layer➡Merge Down (Command-E) [Control-E]. Use the Blur tool to smooth the seam area.

16 Select Filter➡Other➡Offset, again using the same settings (Command-F)[Control-F]. Make the new seam area smooth using the Blur tool. The tile is now seamless. Select➡All. Define the pattern. Create a new file size that you want for your finished snakeskin. Mine is 900×900 pixels. Fill with pattern. If the texture looks too hard or sharp, soften it by selecting Filter➡Blur➡Gaussian Blur, and setting a Radius of about 1.0.

205

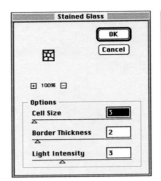

17 You still need to create the scales. A snake's scales are vaguely hexagonal and honeycombed, but give the impression of occurring in a straight line. The method to create the scales works only at the exact sizes and settings that I used. You can enlarge the result, however, with little difficulty. Create a new file 20 pixels square. Switch to default colors. Select Filter➡ Texture➡Stained Glass (Cell Size: 3, Border Thickness: 2, Light Intensity: 3).

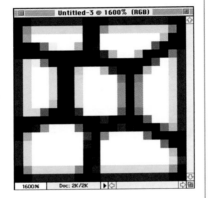

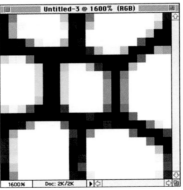

18 Magnify the image to 1600%. Switch the foreground/background colors. Use a small Paintbrush and remove the border areas of the image, leaving the honeycomb alone.

19 Select Filter➡Other➡Offset (Wrap Around, Horizontal: 10, Vertical: 10). Touch up the seams where needed. Select Image➡Image Size, and increase the image size to 40×40 pixels.

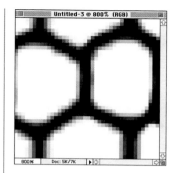

20 Select➡All. Define the pattern. Make the snakeskin background image active. Create a new layer. Fill with pattern. Select Filter➡Blur➡ Gaussian Blur. I used a Radius of 1.2.

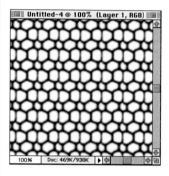

21 Change the blending mode to Hard Light. Choose Filter➡ Stylize➡Emboss (Angle: –67°, Height: 3 pixels, Amount: 100). Now, depending on your partiality to snakes, you can create either a slithering beastie—or a piece of luggage! ■

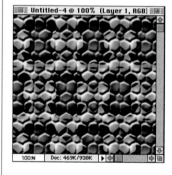

207

Striped patterns provide a good base for design. You can combine them in infinite ways and make them into plaids or diamond patterns for even more variety.

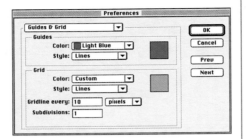

1 Create a new file 10 pixels wide × 100 pixels high. Select File➡ Preferences➡Guides & Grid. Set the Gridlines every 10 pixels with 1 subdivision. Turn on the Grid (Command-")[Control-"]. Turn on Snap to Grid (Shift-Command-") [Shift-Control-"].

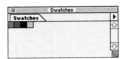

2 Create a palette of 4 colors. I selected light gray, gold, medium blue, and deep rust. Switch the foreground color to the lightest color (light gray).

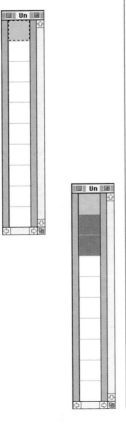

3 Select the rectangular Marquee and set the fixed size to 10 pixels wide × 10 pixels high. Drag the Marquee to the top of the image. Fill the selection with the foreground color.

4 Switch the foreground color to your second color (I used gold). Select the next 2 grid squares (after making first selection, press the Shift key and select the next square). Fill with the foreground color.

5 Follow the chart to complete the rest of the stripe:

Next 3 grid squares: medium blue

Next 1 grid square: rust

Next 1 grid square: light gray

Next 1 grid square: gold

Next 1 grid square: medium blue

6 Hide the grid (Command-") [Control-"]. Create Layer 0. Select Image➡Canvas Size (10 pixels wide, 190 pixels high, Anchor: top center square).

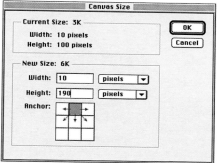

7 Duplicate Layer 0. Select Layer➡Transform➡Flip Vertical. Select Filter➡Other➡Offset (Horizontal: 0, Vertical: 90, Wrap around). Flatten the image. You have a stripe that is symmetrical from the center.

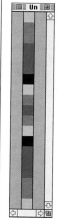

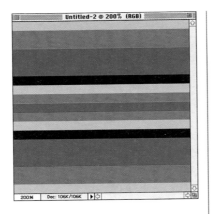

8 Choose Image➡Image Size. Uncheck Constrain Proportions. Check Resample Image. Change the Interpolation Method to Nearest Neighbor. Change the width to 190 pixels and leave the height at 190 pixels. Press OK.

9 Select➡All. Define the pattern. Create a new file at the desired size. Fill with pattern.

VARIATIONS

Basic Faux Plaid

If you want to create a false plaid, duplicate the Background layer of the image in Step 9. Select Layer➡Transform➡Rotate 90° CW. Change the blending mode to Overlay…

...or Color Burn...

...or Difference.

Experiment with all of the blending modes.

Diamonds

You can create interlocked diamonds from your finished stripe.

1 Select Image➡Duplicate. Convert the image to a new mode— Indexed Color mode (Exact palette). This enables you to create a diagonal stripe that does not anti-alias. Select Image➡Rotate Canvas➡Arbitrary (45°).

2 Show the rulers (Command-R) [Control-R]. Add a horizontal and vertical guide in the center of the image. If you magnify the image to 500%, you can see to place the guides on the exact pixel.

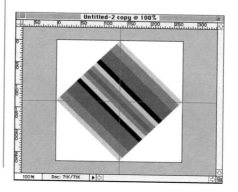

211

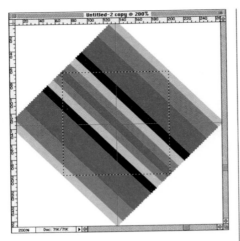

3 Double-click the rectangular Marquee tool and set the Style to Normal with a Feather of 0. Hold the (Shift-Option)[Shift-Alt] keys and place the cursor at the intersection of the two guides. Click and drag out a square marquee that is as large as possible but only contains the stripes (no background).

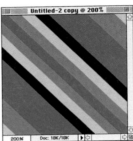

4 Select Image➡Crop.

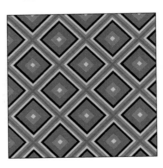

5 Convert the image to RGB mode. Make the tile seamless using the Mosaic method. Select➡All. Define the pattern. Create a new file of the desired size. Fill with pattern.

Try adding some embossing and depth to the diamond repeat. Create a new channel (Channel 4). Fill with the diamond pattern. Choose Image➡Adjust➡Auto Levels. Return to the composite channel. Select Filter➡Render➡ Lighting Effects and use the Stripe Lights preset from the *Photoshop Textures Magic* CD-ROM or duplicate the settings shown.

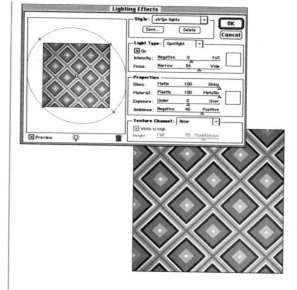

TIP You may not remember the Fibonacci series from high school math, but it is the secret to successful stripes. Stripes that use the numbers in the progression will always be pleasing. The Fibonacci series starts with the numbers 1 and 2. Each of the following numbers is equal to the sum of the preceding two numbers (1, 2, 3, 5, 8, 13, 21, and so on). If you create your stripes so that they use these proportions, they will always work. You can start with 1 pixel, 1 inch, or one foot— the principle remains the same. ■

213

Stucco has so many uses—it can be applied to houses, walls, and Web pages. Although most noisy, embossed, and blurred textures are called stuccos, this effect actually creates one type of plaster pattern that you might see on a neighbor's house. You can vary it in an almost infinite number of ways.

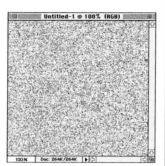

1 Create a new file. This pattern tiles, so you really only need a file as large as one tile. Mine is 300 pixels square so that my tile is one inch when printed. Select Filter➡Noise➡Add Noise (Distribution: Gaussian, Monochromatic). I used an Amount of 100.

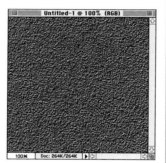

2 Choose Filter➡Stylize➡Emboss (Angle: 130°, Height: 2 pixels, Amount: 100).

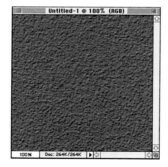

3 Select Filter➡Blur➡Gaussian Blur. I used a Radius of 0.9. The purpose is simply to remove the hard edges—not to blur the texture beyond recognition.

4 Select Image➡Adjust➡Auto Levels.

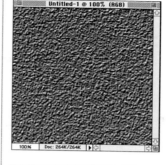

5 Choose Filter➡Fade➡Auto Levels. Did you know that you can Fade any of the Image➡Adjust commands? Leave the opacity at 100%, but change the Mode to Color Burn. This leaves a wonderful texture that almost resembles coal.

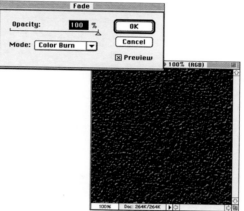

6 Select Filter➡Stylize➡Emboss. Change the Angle to −45° but leave the other settings alone.

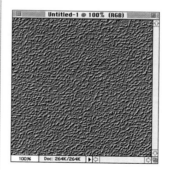

215

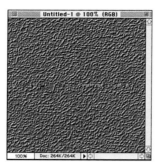

7 Now, you need to add the swirl of the brush to this texture. Select Filter➡Other➡Offset (Wrap Around). Make the Horizontal and Vertical distances one-half of image dimensions. As an added bonus, it makes the texture seamless, although it was practically seamless anyway.

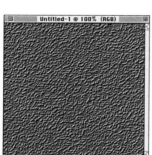

8 Choose Filter➡Distort➡Twirl. I used an Angle of 50°. This is gentle enough to swirl the texture without mangling it.

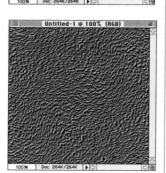

9 Select Filter➡Other➡Offset (Wrap Around). Reuse the last settings. Choose Filter➡Distort➡ Twirl, and use the same settings again. This twirls both seam lines in the image, gives good texture, and keeps the tile seamless.

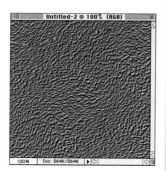

10 In order to keep this texture seamless, you need to finish it in repeat (so that the edges of the texture do not get compromised when the other filters are applied). Select➡All. Define the pattern. Create a new file three times your tile size. Mine is 900×900 pixels for my 300-pixel tile. Fill with pattern.

11 Select Filter➡Sketch➡Graphic Pen (Light/Dark Balance: 50). I used a Stroke Length of 15 and a Direction of Right Diagonal. This makes a wonderful criss-crossed light and dark texture.

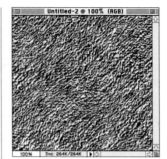

12 Choose Filter➡Stylize➡Emboss (Angle: 138°, Height: 2 pixels, Amount: 100).

13 Select Filter➡Blur➡Gaussian Blur. I used a Radius of 0.9. Again, this is just to soften the hard edge.

14 Double-click the rectangular Marquee. Set the fixed size to the same dimensions as your original tile. Drag the Marquee near the center of the image. Define the pattern.

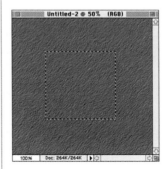

217

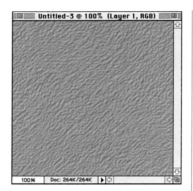

15 Create a new file the same size as your original tile. Decide upon a base color for the stucco. I chose a light peach. Switch the foreground color to the desired color. Fill with foreground color. Create a new layer. Fill the selection with pattern. Change the blending mode to Luminosity. Reduce the layer opacity to about 50%.

16 Select➡All. Define the pattern. Create a new file to the finished size needed. Fill with pattern.

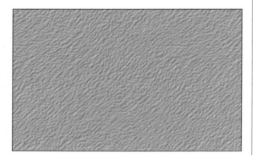

VARIATIONS

If you want a different color stucco, switch the foreground color to whatever color you want. Make the Background layer active for your finished tile. Fill with foreground color. Complete as in Step 16.

To add stronger highlights and shadows, select Image➡Adjust➡Levels. Move the left and right Input sliders to the start of the values on the histogram. If you want to make the texture a bit shinier, move the Gamma (midpoint) slider to the right. If you want to make the texture look as if it is in brighter sunlight, move the Gamma slider to the left.

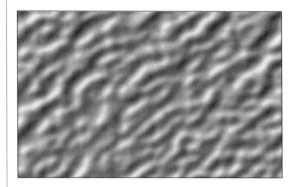

Try making a tile that is more angular and somewhat sharper. In Step 11, select Filter➡Artistic➡Poster Edges. I used an Edge Thickness of 2, an Edge Intensity of 1, and a Posterization of 2. Omit Step 13. ■

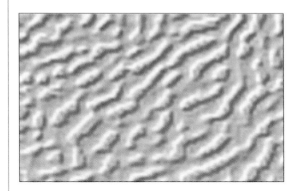

If you are tired of seeing endless "noise" patterns or loud repeats that obscure the text you are trying to read on the Web, here is a no-fail method of generating a seamless tile that is always soft enough to read through. It works with any source image that you can give it—a piece of stock photography or color that you have blobbed onto a file. Let's try it using an image donated by Vivid Details for the *Photoshop Textures Magic* CD-ROM. Best of all, it is never the same twice—it is as individual as your thumbprint.

1 Open the file MM_0248.TIF in the Vivid Details folder on the *Photoshop Textures Magic* CD-ROM, or you can use your own example if you prefer. The starting photo can have an influence on the colors of the final image, but the subject matter of the image is of no importance at all and will not be seen.

2 Double-click the rectangular Marquee tool and set the fixed size to your desired tile size. I used 300×300 pixels.

3 Drag the Marquee into the image anywhere you want. Select Image➡ Crop. Save the file under a new name.

4 Switch to default colors. Fill with background color (white).

5 Double-click the Rubber Stamp tool. Select the Impressionist option, and adjust the other settings as you see them here. Select the 100-pixel soft brush.

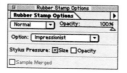

6 The Impressionist version of the Rubber Stamp tool pulls color out of your saved file. It does not pull detail—especially using such a large brush size. Brush the saved color all over your image. You have some control over the color that appears—each time you start and stop, the color changes. Brush with short, choppy strokes.

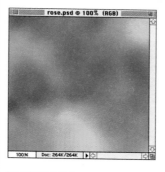

7 For this effect to work, you need to make the tile seamless. Select Filter➧Other➧Offset (Wrap Around), and make the settings approximately one-third of the tile size. I offset the image by 100 pixels in each direction. This is different from the "normal" seamless wrap.

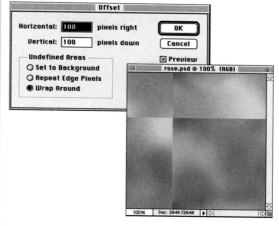

8 You need to cover the hard edge. Don't worry if you have to go to the edges of the image. Continue to use the Impressionist Rubber Stamp tool and the 100-pixel brush (you will need to decrease the size of the brush if your image is smaller). Because you have offset the image, different colors will appear as you brush over the seams. This is good—it helps to move the colors around a bit.

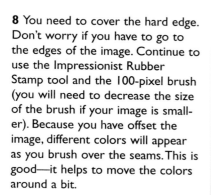

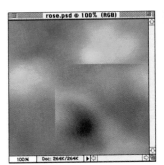

9 Select Filter➡Other➡Offset again with the same settings (Command-F)[Control-F]. Look carefully at this image. This time, the seam line is not quite as sharp and is much less noticeable at the edges.

10 Repair the seam line as you did in Step 8. Only brush over the seam line. Try not to get any closer to the edges than you absolutely must in order to repair the hard edge. Reapply the Offset filter (Command-F)[Control-F]. Continue this cycle of repair and offset until you no longer see a seam line when the image is offset. It takes between 3 and 5 applications of the repair-and-offset cycle to get a totally seamless tile.

11 Select➡All. Define the pattern.

12 Next comes the magic! In order to get a totally seamless tile in the end, you need to create a file that is *three times* your current file size. Create a new file. I created one that is 900×900 pixels (300 pixels × 3). Fill with pattern.

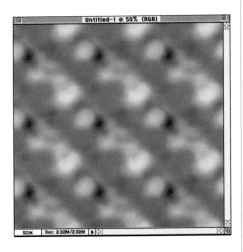

13 Choose Filter➡Stylize➡Find Edges.

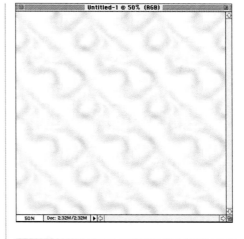

14 Choose Filter➡Blur➡Gaussian Blur. You need to set the Radius high enough for the image to almost completely blur out. You should still be able, however, to see slight variations in color. I used a Radius of 30, but some images have required a Gaussian Blur Radius as high as 63. The size that you select for the Radius determines the amount of detail in the final image.

15 Select Filter➡Stylize➡Find Edges. The image will look blank.

16 Choose Image➡Adjust➡Auto Levels. A fine line pattern appears— and it *is* a pattern. Because you developed this from a seamless tile, the center of the image contains an area that can form a seamless repeat.

223

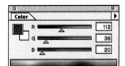

17 Switch the foreground color to whatever color tone you would like your finished pattern to be. Select a color that is at least a middle value or darker. I chose a dark orange-brown.

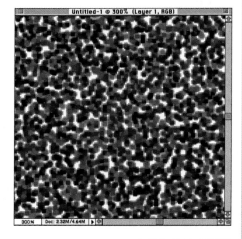

18 Create a new layer (Layer 1). Fill with foreground color. Choose Filter➠Pixelate➠Pointillize. I selected a Cell size of 5. The size that you select has a major impact on the final tile.

19 Duplicate Layer 1. Change the blending mode to Color.

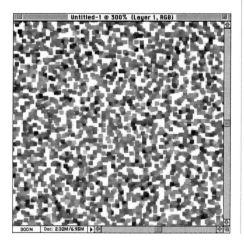

20 Make Layer 1 active. Change the blending mode to Hard Light.

21 Select Filter➥Stylize➥Emboss. The settings that I used here make a good place to start. You are more likely to want to decrease the Height and Amount than you are to increase them.

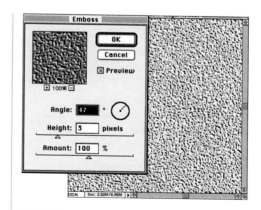

22 The pattern that you worked so hard to create is now totally obscured. You could leave Layer 1 in Hard Light mode and decrease the opacity of the layer, but I prefer to change the blending mode to Multiply at this point and reduce the layer opacity to about 30%.

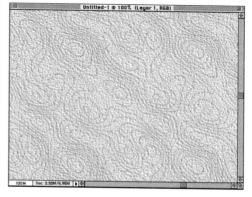

23 You might also want to reduce the opacity of the Layer 1 copy— a setting of 85% is usually enough to remove the "funny" colors produced by the Color blending mode.

225

24 Finally, drag the fixed-size rectangular Marquee near the center of the image. It does not need to be exact, but it does need to be in the center area.

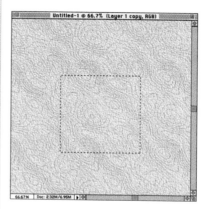

25 Select Image➡Crop. Flatten the image. Convert the image to a new mode—the Indexed Color mode (Web, 216 colors, Diffusion Dither). Save the file as a GIF. The pattern is totally seamless and can be used as a Web background pattern (or for whatever other use you may find). If you want to make the tile smaller, reduce the image size (Image➡ Image Size) *before* you change it to Indexed Color mode.

VARIATIONS

If you want the fine edges to be stronger and more noticeable, after Step 23, make the Background layer active. Select Image➡Adjust➡Levels and move the left Input slider to the right until you like the new image. I prefer to move it only until the Gamma slider (the middle slider) reaches image data, as you can see in the dialog box here.

A larger Gaussian Blur makes the pattern much larger. Here, I used a Gaussian Blur of 63 in Step 14. The base tile was the same.

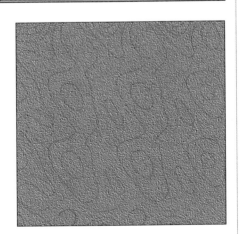

Here it is with a Gaussian blur of 45. The pattern is larger than the original, but not nearly as simple and large as the blur of 63 produces.

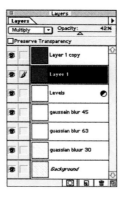

TIP **You can experiment easily with a number of different settings by duplicating the Background layer a few times and using different Gaussian blur settings. Complete Steps 15 and 16 for each layer. If you then complete Steps 17–23 at the top of the layer list, you have a file that you can play with and hide and show layers, change opacities and blending modes, and so on. Here's the way I structured mine.**

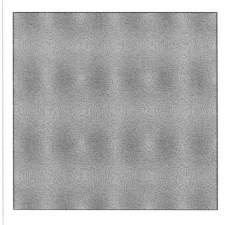

You could make the original photo extract tile seamless using the Rubber Stamp method. This cuts out Steps 4 through 10. However, even at a Gaussian blur of 63 in Step 14, the resulting pattern may be too detailed. This method is faster, but you may want to repeat Steps 13 and 14 twice (Find Edges and Gaussian Blur), using a different setting for Step 14. ▪

227

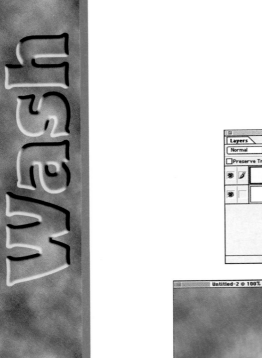

A pattern based on a watercolor wash makes a lovely and unusual Web background. This technique is amazingly simple—but it has many uses and can be varied endlessly by merely changing the colors used.

1 Create a new file. Mine is 400×400 pixels. Switch to default colors. Create a new layer (Layer 1). Switch the foreground color to any dark color that you want. I chose a medium-dark blue.

2 Apply Filter➡Render➡Clouds. Clouds is the only native Photoshop filter that works in a totally blank and transparent image. Reduce the layer opacity to about 90%.

3 Create a new layer (Layer 2). Switch the foreground color to a much lighter color. I used a medium-light green.

4 Reapply the Clouds filter (Command-F)[Control-F]. Reduce the layer opacity to 50%.

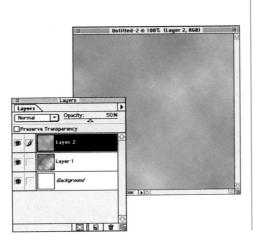

5 Create a new layer (Layer 3). Switch the foreground color to a strong color that is not already in the image. I used a strong red. Switch the background color to another dark color—a color that is almost the complement of the foreground color seems to work best. I chose a deep, dull green.

6 Reapply the Clouds filter (Command-F)[Control-F]. Change the blending mode of the layer to Overlay.

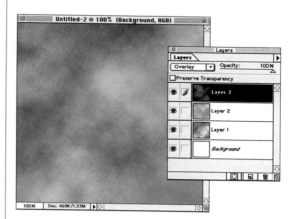

7 Make the Background layer active. Choose Filter→Noise→Add Noise (Gaussian, do not check Monochromatic). Use a large amount—until you can see it through the other textures. I used an Amount of 700.

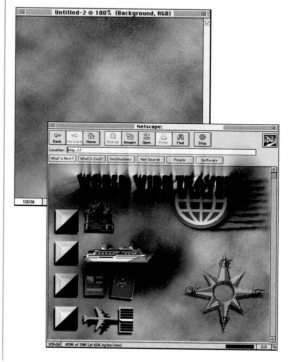

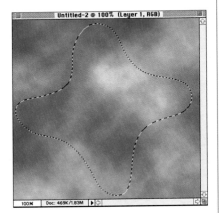

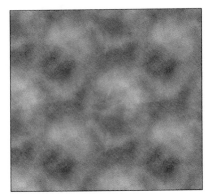

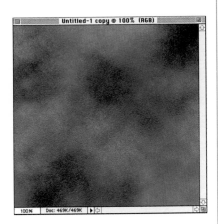

VARIATIONS

If you want to make the texture seamless, you need to make each layer seamless after you apply the Clouds filter—and before you change the layer opacity or change the blending mode. Each time that you apply the Clouds filter, make the pattern seamless using the Rubber Stamp method. This is only partially successful because it is hard to use the Rubber Stamp tool on the Clouds filter. After you do the best job that you can—especially on the areas at the edges of the image, select the Lasso tool. Draw a selection in the shape of a fat cross around the area where the Offset filter joined the original corners of the image. Choose Select➥Feather, and pick a large feather. I used 15 pixels. Reapply the Clouds filter to the selection. It will blend perfectly. You do not need to make the Background layer seamless. When all three clouds layers are seamless, define the pattern, and use it to fill a new image with pattern.

To create a different color range, you can select Image➥Duplicate (Merged Layers Only) and then invert the result (Command-I) [Control-I].

You can also change the opacities of the layers to change the look of the watercolor wash. I changed Layer 1 to 82% opacity and Layer 2 to 14% opacity.

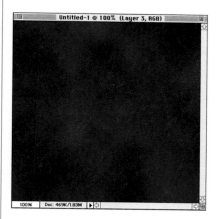

You can change the blending mode on Layer 3. I set it to Luminosity mode.

Of course, you can try a totally different color scheme as well. I used a light yellow for Layer 1, a deeper red for Layer 2, and a very dark blue and maroon for Layer 3.

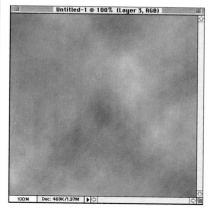

231

If you want more, the "Leather" effect (page 120) shows you another technique using the Clouds filter. ■

Still water may run deep, but turbulent water is more fun to design. This effect allows you to play creator to ponds and rivers and streams—in sun or in storm.

1 Create a new file. You will be able to tile this, but you should use a tile size as large as practicality allows to give the water the maximum variety. My file is 300×300 pixels—but you will be happier with the results if you use a tile of at least 400×600 pixels. Switch the foreground color to a "watery" blue. I used RGB: 0, 138, 183. The color is not extremely critical because you can easily change it afterwards. Fill the image with foreground color.

2 Create a new layer (Layer 1). Switch the foreground color to a deeper sea blue. I used RGB: 0, 92, 120. Fill Layer 1 with the foreground color. Create a layer mask.

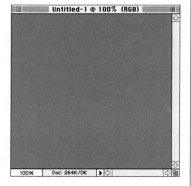

3 Gee, that looks boring! So far, we have one color on top of another and a layer mask that does nothing. Never fear…the effect is actually built in the layer mask. Switch to default colors (your colors should already be showing black and white while the layer mask is selected). Choose Filter➡Render➡Clouds. Finally, you can see something happening other than a solid color!

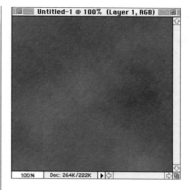

4 Select Filter➡Render➡ Difference Clouds. Reapply this filter (Command-F)[Control-F] several times (2 or 3 is enough). Each time you reapply the Difference Clouds filter, you are adding internal complexity to the clouds—even if the difference is not visible onscreen. Shown here is just the layer mask (which, of course, is grayscale).

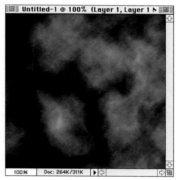

5 Choose Filter➡Stylize➡Find Edges. Invert the image (Command-I)[Control-I]. The layer mask is pictured here because the effect is still too light to be printable. (Your screen will show the effect rather than the layer mask.)

233

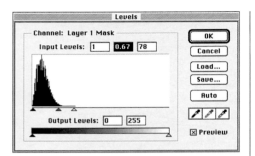

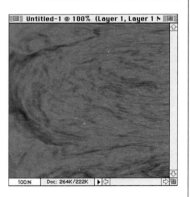

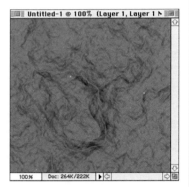

6 Select Image➥Adjust➥Levels. Position the right Input slider at the right edge of the data in the Histogram. Move the Gamma (middle) slider to the right until it is near the area where the data curve flattens. This removes much of the layer mask detail and darkens what is left. Change the blending mode to Multiply.

7 Select Image➥Rotate Canvas➥ 90° CW. Apply Filter➥Distort➥ Polar Coordinates (Polar to Rectangular). Select Image➥Rotate Canvas➥90° CCW. This adds a linearity that is characteristic of water.

8 The Polar Coordinates filter always leaves some curved shapes and lines on the left side of the image (if you rotated the image as I did). This needs to be removed if the image is to resemble water. Double-click the rectangular Marquee tool and set the Style to Normal and the Feather to 0. Select the entire area to the right of the curved stuff. Choose Layer➡Transform➡Free Transform (Command-T)[Control-T]. Place your cursor on the center control point on the left edge of the selected area and drag the point to the left edge of the image. This stretches the "good" part of the layer mask over the entire image. Double-click inside of the selection to execute the transformation. Deselect.

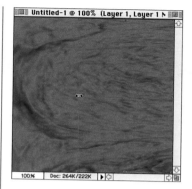

9 This looks much more like water, but it may still be too light. The easy way to darken the image is to use the Levels command and move the right Input slider to the left. That is a permanent move, however, and cannot be changed later. I prefer maximum editability. Therefore, load the layer mask of Layer 1 by pressing the (Command)[Control] key and clicking on the layer mask thumbnail in the Layers palette. Create a Levels adjustment layer with a blending mode of Multiply. Click OK in the Levels dialog box without making any changes. If it is still not dark enough, you can always duplicate the adjustment layer.

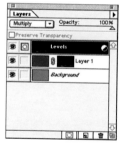

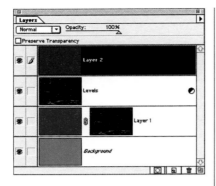

10 The water needs highlights. Create a new layer (Layer 2). Switch the foreground color to a contrasting color for highlights. I used a strong green—RGB: 30, 85, 31. Fill with foreground color. Now the image is solid green. But not for long…

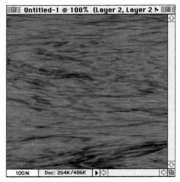

11 Create a layer mask. Repeat Steps 3 through 8 in the Layer 2 layer mask. A slightly different pattern will form. When you repeat Step 6, select Screen mode rather than Multiply.

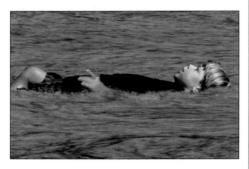

12 Load the layer mask of Layer 2 by pressing the (Command) [Control] key and clicking on the layer mask thumbnail in the Layers palette. Create a Levels adjustment layer with a blending mode of Screen. Click OK in the Levels dialog box without making any changes.

VARIATIONS

If you want to see the green
streaks in the water, duplicate Layer
2. Position the layer at the top
of the Layers list. Make the layer
mask active. You can redo Steps 3
through 8 to create a different layer
mask, or you can take the easy way
out and select Layer➡Transform➡
Flip Horizontal to simply reposition
the layer mask to let the original
Layer 2 show through. Leave the
Blending mode in Normal. Load the
layer mask of Layer 2 copy by
pressing the (Command)[Control]
key and clicking on the layer mask
thumbnail in the Layers palette.
Create a Levels Adjustment layer.
Leave the Mode in Normal and
move the Input sliders where you
want them to bring out the values
in the image.

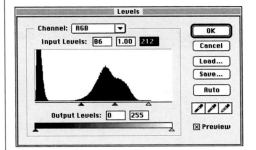

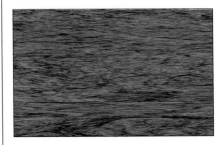

To create the ocean on a cloudy—
almost stormy—day, make the
background layer active in the finished image. Switch the foreground
color to a gray. I used RGB: 142,
142, 142. Fill the Background layer
with the foreground color. You can
leave the other layers alone or
adjust or recolor them as well. You
can also create additional layers to
bring in streaks of other colors
(following Steps 2 through 9 to
do so).

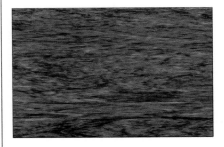

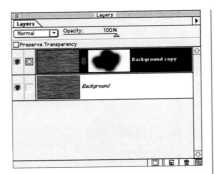

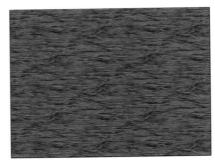

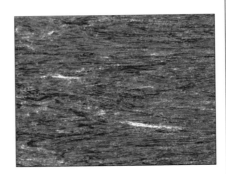

You can make the water tile seamlessly. After you have your finished tile, select Image➡Duplicate (Merged Layers only). Duplicate the Background layer. Select Filter➡ Other➡Offset (Wrap Around). Make the Horizontal and Vertical distances one-half of image dimensions. Create a layer mask. Use a hard 100-pixel paintbrush and black. Paint out the center area of the image in the layer mask leaving only the area around the rim. Try not to fog the tile (that is why I recommend a fairly hard brush). Select➡All. Make sure that the layer—*not* the layer mask—is active. Define the pattern. Create a new file to the desired size. Fill with pattern. You will get the best results using a rectangular rather than a square tile, and using a fairly large tile size. Water is supposed to be completely random. If you notice the same formations multiple times, the incongruity becomes distracting. You can use the layer mask to also help remove the most obvious sections of the repeat. Simply paint on the layer mask to pick up detail from the other image. It may take a few tries to get it right.

Try making sparkling highlights in the water. Create a new layer at the top of the Layers list. Fill with white. Repeat Steps 2 through 8 to create a new layer mask texture. In Step 6, leave the blending mode at Normal. When you are finished, set the levels as you want and change the blending mode to Dissolve. This sprinkles tiny, too-sharp dots on the water. Create a new layer. Position the layer below the sparkles highlights layer. Make the sparkles layer active. Merge down

(Command-E)[Control-E]. This keeps the Dissolve mode dots in a Normal mode layer (in other words, this layer now just contains the sparkles, some transparency, and no layer mask). Select Filter➡ Blur➡Gaussian Blur (0.9 or other small amount).

Now, try changing the water into tree bark. Select Image➡Rotate Canvas 90° CW. Make the Background layer active. Switch the foreground color to a shade of "tree" brown. I used RGB: 79, 59, 42. Fill the Background layer with foreground color. The green layer needs to be changed as well (Layer 2, in the original example). Change it to a shade of orange/brown (I used RGB: 135, 66, 11). Change the blending mode to Overlay. For additional realism, (Option) [Alt] Merge Visible to a new layer. Select Image➡Adjust➡Desaturate (Shift-Command-U)[Shift-Control-U]. Choose Image➡Adjust➡Auto Levels. Change the blending mode to Hard Light. Choose Filter➡ Stylize➡Emboss (Angle: 127°, Height: 4 pixels, Amount: 50). If the embossing looks too "perfect," select Layer➡Transform➡Flip Horizontal (or Vertical or Rotate 180°) to move the embossing. If you want, Select Filter➡Blur➡ Gaussian Blur (0.9 or less) to soften the embossing.

If you want more textures that you can create in a layer mask, try "Rocks" (page 176). ■

Wicker

You probably did not expect a Photoshop book to introduce you to Basket Weaving 101. Wicker and other types of natural-fiber basket weaves, however, have a long and honorable history. The textures that they create have been copied and imitated in many different media— why not the electronic one? Besides, with the wonder of Photoshop, you only have to create a tiny piece of the basket.

1 Create a new file 86 pixels wide × 24 pixels high. This file is for the wicker fiber. Magnify the image to 500%. Switch the foreground color to a medium earth tone. I selected RGB: 185, 161, 87. Create a new layer. Fill with foreground color.

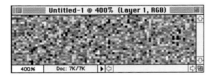

2 Select Filter➡Noise➡Add Noise (Distribution: Gaussian, Monochromatic Off). I used an Amount of 135.

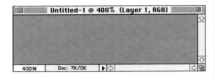

3 Apply Filter➡Blur➡Motion Blur. I used an Angle of 20° and a Distance of 33. You are creating the "twist" in the fiber, and the bits of noise from Step 2 are the range of colors that are twisted into the fiber.

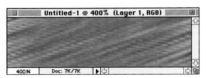

4 Create a new layer. Choose the Pencil tool and the 1-pixel brush. Switch foreground/background colors so that you can keep the wicker color in the toolbox. Switch the foreground color to black. Paint some random short lines on the image.

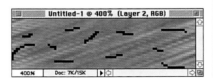

5 Reapply Filter➡Blur➡Motion Blur (Command-F)[Control-F]. This puts a little bit of shadow detail into the fiber.

6 Create a new layer. Fill with background color. Reduce the layer opacity to about 35%. You just want to influence the color of the fiber a bit—not obliterate all of the work you just put into it.

7 Create a new layer. Double-click on the Gradient tool and select the Center High gradient preset from the *Photoshop Textures Magic* CD-ROM. Change the Type to Linear. Drag the Gradient cursor from the top of the image to the bottom, and press the Shift key to constrain the direction. Wicker material is round, and you have just added that roundness to your image.

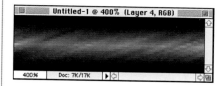

8 This next step is tricky. The two horizontal ends of the image are going to "virtually" sink under the vertical strands of fiber to either side. Therefore, the ends need to be darker than the center of the file. However, if you make the ends too dark, the illusion of roundness disappears. Change the Gradient to Foreground to Transparent. Create a new layer. Turn on the Rulers (Command-R)[Control-R]. Add a Horizontal guide at the 12-pixel mark on the side ruler (the halfway point). Place the Gradient cursor in the upper-left corner of the image, press the Shift key, and drag the cursor diagonally until it reaches the guide. Then place the Gradient cursor in the lower-right corner of the image, press the Shift key, and drag the cursor diagonally until it reaches the guide. Now, the two corners are gently shadowed. If you want a slightly stronger shadow, reapply the Gradient to the top-left corner (over the first one).

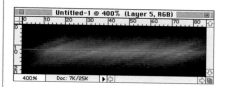

241

9 Create a new layer (Layer 6). (Option)[Alt] Merge Visible to the new layer (which should be at the top of the Layers list). Select➦All. Copy.

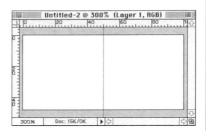

10 Create a new file 100 pixels wide × 48 pixels high. There actually is a logic behind this file size. It needs to be twice the height of the fiber image (24×2=48), and the width of the fiber image plus the width of the vertical fiber that needs to be drawn (86 plus a warp width of 14 pixels=100 pixels). Create a new layer. Turn on the Rulers (Command-R)[Control-R]. Add a Vertical guide at the 50-pixel mark on the top ruler. Enlarge the window so that it is a little bit bigger than the image.

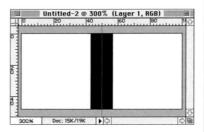

11 Double-click the Line tool. Set the Line Width to 14 pixels and Anti-aliased off. Do not use arrowheads. Place your cursor on the guideline at the bottom of the window outside of the image. Press the Shift key and drag the line vertically up the guide. Release when it is outside of the image again. This ensures that the line covers the entire image.

12 Switch to default colors. Double-click the Gradient tool. Choose the Center white Gradient preset from the *Photoshop Textures Magic* CD-ROM. Set the Gradient opacity to 30% and the mode to Normal. Turn on Preserve Transparency. Position the Gradient cursor exactly at the left edge of the line and drag it exactly to the right edge of the line. Press the Shift key as you drag to create a perfectly straight Gradient. This gives depth and roundness to the vertical wicker fiber.

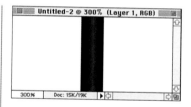

13 Paste the fiber swatch that you copied in Step 9 into the new image. As long as you have nothing selected in the image, the horizontal fiber will paste in the exact center of the file. Select Layer➡Merge Down (Command-E)[Control-E]. This makes one row of wicker weaving.

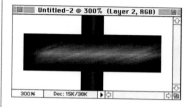

14 Duplicate Layer 1. Select Filter➡Other➡Offset (Horizontal: 50, Vertical: 24, Wrap Around). These distances are one-half of image dimensions. This gives you a perfect staggered repeat, and simulates a true under-and-over weave.

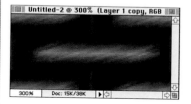

243

15 Select➡All. Define the pattern. Create a new file of the desired dimensions. Mine is 750×750 pixels. Fill the new image with pattern.

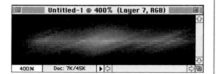

VARIATIONS

Highlighted Wicker

If you want the wicker to look as if it is bending a little as it goes over the vertical fiber, you need to highlight the center of the weft fiber and shadow the ends more deeply. To do this, you need to add some new steps after Step 8. Press the (Option)[Alt] key as you create a new layer. In the Layer Options dialog box, select Soft Light mode and check the Fill with Soft-Light-neutral color (50% gray) box. Double-click the Toning tool and select the Dodge tool at 12% exposure. Select Midtones as the mode. Use a soft, fairly large brush and lighten the center of the fiber in a somewhat diagonal direction that follows the angle of the fiber "twist."

To add additional shadowing, create a new layer. Double-click the Gradient tool. Change the Gradient to Foreground to Transparent. Set the Gradient opacity to 30%. Place the Gradient cursor in the upper-left corner of the image, press the Shift key, and drag the cursor diagonally until it reaches the bottom of the image. Repeat two more times. Then, place the Gradient cursor in the lower-right corner of the image, press the Shift key, and drag the cursor diagonally until it reaches the top of the image. Do this a total of three times. Your fiber now has almost a lozenge shape. From this point, follow Steps 9 to the end of the original instructions.

Curved Wicker

To add a real curve to the wicker fiber, make these changes after Step 13. Turn off Preserve Transparency. Choose Image➡Rotate Canvas➡ 90° CW. Apply Filter➡Distort➡ Shear and create a center curve similar to the one shown.

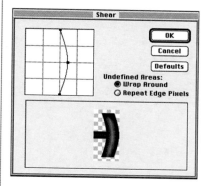

Then complete Step 14. However, the points that you can see here...

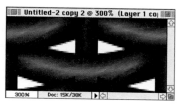

...need to be "tucked behind" the fiber on the row above. Create a layer mask. Use black and a soft brush and brush out the points. Return to the composite channel or you will not be able to define the pattern.

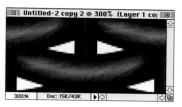

Then finish according to the original instructions. This makes a very open wicker texture. ■

Woodgrain is a very useful texture for backgrounds, three-dimensional work, and as paneling. This wood technique creates a grainy wood that is characteristic of walnut. It is also a seamless pattern. It is much easier to make if you don't worry about tiling it, but it looks great tiled!

1 Create a new file. I used one 300×300 pixels. If you need this texture for printed work, create it at 72 dpi and scale up to 300 dpi later using nearest neighbor interpolation. Switch the foreground color to a deep brown (I used RGB: 75, 30, 14). Switch the background color to a lighter brown (I used RGB: 132, 86, 50). Fill with background color.

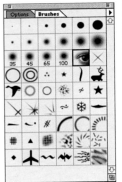

2 Load the Assorted Brushes into the Brushes palette. They are located inside of the (Photoshop/Goodies/Brushes & Patterns folder) [Photoshop/Brushes directory]. Select the brush that looks like an eye.

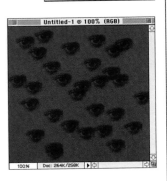

3 Choose the Paintbrush tool and stamp the brush in a random manner all over your image.

4 Choose Filter➡Blur➡Motion Blur. I used an Angle of −18° and a Distance of 44 pixels.

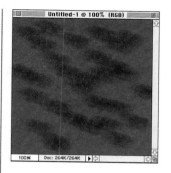

5 We need to make the background seamless. Choose Filter➡Other➡Offset set at half of your file size in each direction, Wrap Around.

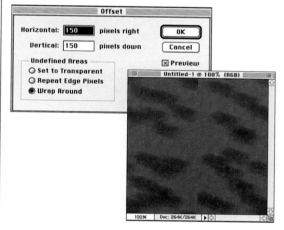

6 Dab some additional "eyes" on the areas that seem to need it. Repeat Step 4.

247

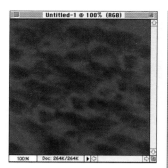

7 Apply Filter➡Other➡Offset at the same settings as before to put the background into its original position. You will probably see a slight line across the center. Make the pattern seamless using the Rubber Stamp method. You can really mix up the color areas as you work. Just be careful not to get too close to the sides of the image.

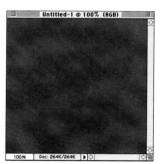

8 Choose Filter➡Blur➡Gaussian Blur. Smooth out the Background. I used a Radius of 5.4. Don't over-smooth it—if you don't smooth it enough, you can fix it later.

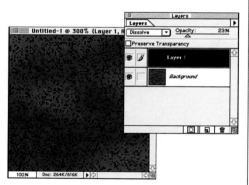

9 Wood generally has grain and noise in it. Let's add some noise that uses the colors in our image. Create a new layer. Fill with fore-ground color. Change the blending mode to Dissolve, and reduce the layer opacity until you like the amount of noise. I used 23%.

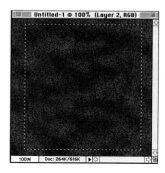

10 Now it's time to create the wood grain. Create a new layer. The grain needs to be seamless, so select the rectangular Marquee and set the fixed size to 250 pixels wide × 275 pixels high. Drag the Marquee into the center of the image. This way, it is easier not to draw woodgrain on the entire layer.

11 Choose the Paintbrush tool and a small, soft brush. This is a good place to vary pressure if you have a pressure-sensitive tablet. Draw any shaped woodgrain lines that you like. Many types of wood tend to have narrow rings horizontally whereas the vertical spaces are more generous.

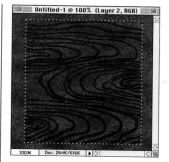

12 Deselect. Apply Filter➡Other➡ Offset. Continue to use the same settings as before. You can clearly see where it is necessary to join the lines.

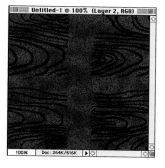

13 Connect the lines as best you can. Sometimes, you may want to use the Eraser tool if you cannot get an area to join.

14 Here's how to narrow the distance between the growth rings. Turn on the rulers (Command-R) [Control-R]. Add a Horizontal guide from the top ruler to the halfway mark on the vertical rule (I placed mine at the 150 pixel mark).

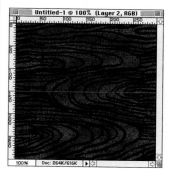

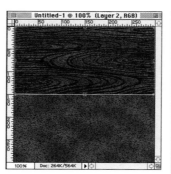

15 Use the Free Transform command (Command-T)[Control-T] to scale the image by bringing the center-bottom point up to the guide. Double-click inside the shape to execute the scaling function.

16 Duplicate Layer 3. Apply Filter➡ Other➡Offset. By using the same settings, you move the copied layer down to the other half of the image and wrap it from side to side as well. The pattern should still be seamless. Merge Down (Command-E)[Control-E]. Touch up as needed to make the image seamless if there is a matching problem. You might also want to try using the Masked Offset method of making an image seamless if you cannot get the wood to join any other way.

17 Duplicate Layer 2. Choose Filter➡Stylize➡Wind (Blast, From the Left). Make Layer 2 active. Reduce the layer opacity so that the Wind filter changes can appear but you can still see some of the original grain. I used an opacity of 34%.

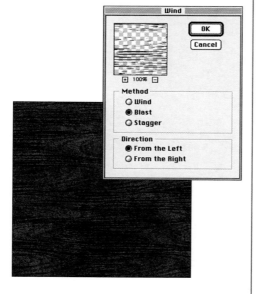

18 When you have finished, tweak the opacity of the Dissolve layer (Layer 1) to control the amount of grain, or the opacities of Layer 2 and Layer 2 copy to fine-tune the effect.

VARIATIONS

A Quick, Non–Repeating Method

If you want a quick wood texture with a stronger grain, you can create a new file and fill with background color (your lighter color). Create a new layer. Fill with foreground color. Change the blending mode to Dissolve, and reduce the layer's opacity as you did in Step 9. Create a new layer and draw your woodgrain lines. Flatten the image. Duplicate the Background layer. Choose Filter➡Blur➡Gaussian Blur and increase the Radius until the image loses focus but is not obliterated. I used a Radius of 2.4. Change the blending mode to Darken. (This gives a subtle glow to the image—like polished wood.) Duplicate the Background layer again. Position the layer at the top of the layer list. Select Filter➡Stylize➡Wind (Blast, From the Left). Reduce the opacity of the layer until you like the results. I used an opacity of 90%.

Weather–Beaten Wood

To create weathered wood, follow the Quick, Non-Repeating method instructions. Change the blending mode for the top layer to Exclusion. I used foreground color RGB: 81, 50, 16, and background color RGB: 163, 125, 23 in the example.

Distressed Wood

You can add dark grain to any finished wood texture very easily. Create a new layer (Layer 1) by holding the (Option)[Alt] key and clicking on the New Layer icon. In the dialog box, change the blending mode to Multiply and check the box marked Fill with Multiply—neutral color (white). Choose Filter➡Noise➡Add Noise (Gaussian, Monochromatic). I used an Amount of 130. Select Filter➡Stylize➡Diffuse (Normal). Reapply this filter as many times as you want until you create clumps of noise (Command-F)[Control-F].

Colorized Wood

Try changing the color of the wood. After your texture is complete (or at a preliminary stage if you want), create an adjustment layer using Hue/Saturation. You can click the Colorize button to make your wood more monochromatic, or not (the "not" option cycles the colors around the color wheel). ■

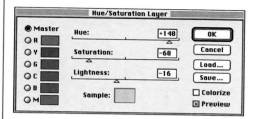

Appendix A

Listing of Contributors

Software and Filters

Adobe Systems, Inc.

345 Park Avenue

San Jose, CA 95110-6000

Phone: 408-536-6000

Fax: 408-537-6000

http://www.adobe.com

Acrobat Reader™ 3.0 (Mac and PC)

Photoshop™ 3.0.5 Tryout (Mac and PC)

After Effects™ 3.0 Tryout (Mac only)

Streamline™ 3.1 Tryout (Mac and PC)

Dimensions™ 2.0 Tryout (Mac only)

Illustrator® 6.0 Tryout (Mac only)

Alien Skin Software

1100 Wake Forest Rd. Suite 101

Raleigh, NC 27604

Phone: 919-832-4124

Fax: 919-832-4065

Eye Candy 3.0 Demo (Mac and PC)

Andromeda Software, Inc.

699 Hampshire Rd. Suite 109

Thousand Oaks, CA 91361

Phone: 800-547-0055 or 805-379-4109

Fax: 805-379-5253

orders@andromeda.com

Series 1,2, 3, & 4 Demos (Mac and PC)

AutoFX

15 North Main Street Suite 8

Wolfeboro, NH 03894

Phone: 603-569-8800

Fax: 603-569-9702

http://www.autofx.com

Sample Edge, Page Effects (Mac and PC)

Sample Patterns and Textures (PC)

255

Cochenille
P.O. Box 4276
Encinitas, CA 92023
Phone: 619-259-1698
Fax: 619-259-3746
info@cochenille.com

StitchPainter (Mac and PC)

Digital Frontiers
1019 Asbury Ave.
Evanston, IL 60202
Phone: 827-328-0880
Fax: 827-869-2053
http://www/digfrontiers.com

HVS Color (Mac and PC)
HVS Photo JPEG (PC)

Extensis
1800 SW First Ave. Suite 500
Portland, OR 97201-5322
Phone: 503-274-2020
Fax: 503-274-0530
http://www.extensis.com

Intellihance (Mac and PC)
PhotoTools (Mac and PC)

Fractal Design, Inc.
5550 Scotts Valley Drive
Scotts Valley, CA 95066
Phone: 408-688-5300
http://www.fractal.com

Detailer (Mac and PC)

Fortune Hill, Inc.
814 Glendover Cove
Lexington, KY 40502
Phone: 606-269-0933
samoore@best.com

Wild River SSK Demo (Mac only)

MetaTools, Inc.
6303 Carpinteria Ave.
Carpinteria, CA 93013
Phone: 805-566-6200
metasales@aol.com

KPT 3.0 Demo (Mac and PC)

Specular, International
7 Pomeroy Lane
Amherst, MA 01002
Phone: 800-433-SPEC
Fax: 413-253-0540

Infini-D™ Demo (Mac and PC)
Collage 2.0 Demo (Mac only)
LogoMotion Demo (Mac only)
TextureScape™ Demo (Mac only)

Three-D Graphics
1801 Avenue of the Stars
Suite 600
Los Angeles, CA 90067-5908
Voice: 310-553-3313
Fax: 310-788-8975
http://www.threedgraphics.com

Texture Creator (Mac and PC)

Vertigo
Phone: 1-888-4-VERTIGO
Fax: 604-684-2108
http://www.vertigo3d.com

3D Dizzy (Mac only)

Xaos Tools, Inc.
55 Hawthorn Suite 1000
San Francisco, CA 94105
Phone: 1-800-BUY-XAOS

Paint Alchemy 2™ Demo (Mac only)
Terrazo 2™ Demo (Mac only)
TypeCaster™ Demo (Mac only)

Stock Images

Artis
Edvard Hartmann Platz 3M12
Laxenburg, Austria
Phone: 43-2236-73570
Fax: 43-2236-73661
http://www.artis.com

Sample images created with Texture
Magic™ (Mac)

DigitalShowbiz
http://www.dsb.com

Sample images from
Ruff Stuff (Mac and PC)

MetaTools, Inc.
6303 Carpinteria Ave.
Carpinteria, CA 93013
Phone: 805-566-6200
metasales@aol.com

257

Ultimate Symbol Collection

31 Wilderness Drive

Stony Point, NY 10980-3447

Phone: 800-611-4761

Fax: 914-942-0004

Vivid Details

8228 Sulphur Mtn. Rd.

Ojai, CA 93023

Phone: 805-646-0021

http://www.vividdetails.com

Appendix B

What's on the CD-ROM

The CD-ROM that comes with this book is both Macintosh and Windows compatible. Please note that there are several demos and tryouts available for Macintosh users that are not available for Windows users, and vice versa. This means that either the product does not exist for that platform, or a version is being created but was not available at the time of publication.

It is suggested that you refer to the READ ME and other information files included in the demo software program's folder. Also, visit the corporate Web sites for updates and more information. (The URLs are noted in Appendix A.) There are often demos of new software available for downloading and tryout.

The CD-ROM is divided into four folders.

Contents

Filters
This folder contains lots of different filters you can use to manipulate your images. You can do a variety of things with filters, one of the most powerful features of Photoshop. These filters are all commercial demos.

Images
Some of the techniques in *Photoshop Textures Magic* begin with stock art provided by commercial stock photo companies. You'll find them here.

Presets
Here's where you'll find the "pieces" referred to in the Toolbox section at the start of many of the techniques. These include the Lighting Styles presets, Gradient presets, and a variety of Curves and Color sets, as well as some templates to use to create marbled patterns.

Software
This folder contains demos of commercial software, including Adobe products and Fractal Design products.

Installation

For detailed instructions on how to install and use the resources I've included on the CD-ROM, please consult the READ ME and ABOUT files in the individual Software, Filters, Presets, and Images folders. General installation information follows:

Filters

Filters should be copied into the Plug-Ins folder, located in the same place as your Adobe Photoshop application. Then, relaunch Photoshop, and find the filters in the Filter menu. You can now access and apply these third-party filters the same way you use Photoshop's filters.

Preset Files

The Lighting Styles presets should be copied into the Lighting FX folder in the Plugins/Filters folder inside of the Photoshop folder or directory.

You can load the other presets through their specific menus (example: the Gradients presets can be loaded into the Gradients list by selecting the Edit button on the Gradient Options palette and then choosing Load… from the Edit dialog box). The files suffixed by .act or .alt are color tables and can be opened either by the Custom option in the Image➡Mode➡Color Table command or by the Load or Replace command in the Swatches palette menu. These files are in the CLUTS subfolder.

.Acv files can be opened by the Levels or Curves commands. .Ahu files may be opened by the Hue/Saturation command. These files are found in the Maps subfolder.

The Images subfolder contains the files that are specifically referred to by the effects in the book. They are all .PSD files (native Photoshop format).

All of the files in all of the subfolders here may be copied to your hard disk if you want.

Stock Imagery and Textures

The stock photos and textures located in the Images folder do not need to be copied to your hard drive. For most files, you can double-click on them to open them in Photoshop. If they do not open, try opening Photoshop first, then select File➡Open. Then choose the file you would like to open. If you particularly like a certain image and would like to access it quickly, by all means copy it to your hard drive.

Gallery

page 30

page 34

page 46

page 52

page 58

page 66

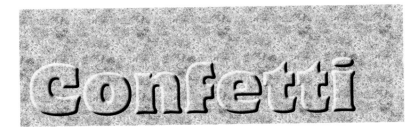

page 92

page 98

page 104

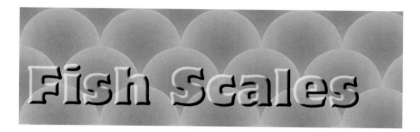

page 108

page 112

page 120

page 124

page 128

page 134

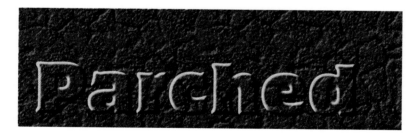

page 162

page 168

page 172

page 176

page 182

page 188

page 214

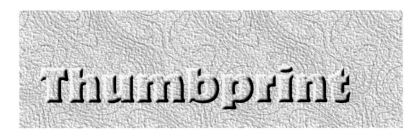

page 220

page 228

page 232

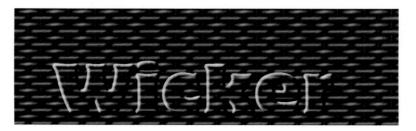

page 240

page 246

Other DESIGN/GRAPHICS Titles

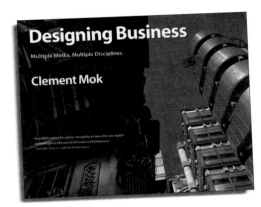

Designing Business

Provides the design/business communities with a new way of thinking about how the right design can be a strategic business advantage. It is the definitive guide to presenting a business identity through the use of traditional media vehicles and emerging technologies.

- CD-ROM (dual-platform) exhibits interactive prototypes of multimedia brochures, interactive television, and Web sites as developed by Clement Mok Designs Inc., one of the most sought after interactive design agencies in the world
- Shows how effective communication is one way to out-think, out-plan, and out-perform the competition

Clement Mok
1-56830-282-7 ■ $60.00 USA/$81.95 CDN
264 pp., 8 x 10, Covers PC and Macintosh, New - Expert
Available Now

Adobe Persuasion: Classroom in a Book
1-56830-316-5 ■ $40.00 USA/$56.95 CDN
Available Now

Learning Adobe FrameMaker
1-56830-290-8 ■ $60.00 USA/$81.95 CDN
Available Now

Adobe Illustrator for Windows: Classroom in a Book
1-56830-053-0 ■ $44.95 USA/$59.99 CDN
Available Now

Adobe PageMaker for Windows: Classroom in a Book
1-56830-184-7 ■ $45.00 USA/$61.95 CDN
Available Now

Adobe Photoshop: Classroom in a Book
1-56830-317-3 ■ $45.00 USA/$63.95 CDN
Available Now

Advanced Adobe PageMaker for Windows 95: Classroom in a Book
1-56830-262-2 ■ $50.00 USA/$68.95 CDN
Available Now

Advanced Adobe Photoshop for Windows: Classroom in a Book
1-56830-116-2 ■ $50.00 USA/$68.95 CDN
Available Now

The Amazing PhotoDeluxe Book for Windows
1-56830-286-X ■ $30.00 USA/$40.95 CDN
Available Now

Branding with Type
1-56830-248-7 ■ $18.00 USA/$24.95 CDN
Available Now

Digital Type Design Guide
1-56830-190-1 ■ $45.00 USA/$61.95 CDN
Available Now

Fractal Design Painter Creative Techniques
1-56830-283-5 ■ $45.00 USA/$56.95 CDN
Available Now

Photoshop 4 Type Magic 1
1-56830-380-7 ■ $39.99 USA/$47.95 CDN
Available Now

Photoshop Web Magic
1-56830-314-9 ■ $45.00 USA/$63.95 CDN
Available Now

Adobe Photoshop Complete
1-56830-323-8 ■ $49.99 USA/$61.95 CDN
Available Now

Stop Stealing Sheep & Find Out How Type Works
0-672-48543-5 ■ $19.95 USA/$26.99 CDN
Available Now

Visit your fine local bookstore, or for more information visit us at http//:www.mcp.com/hayden/

PLUG YOURSELF INTO...

THE MACMILLAN
INFORMATION SUPERLIBRARY™

Free information and vast computer resources from the world's leading computer book publisher—online!

FIND THE BOOKS THAT ARE RIGHT FOR YOU!
A complete online catalog, plus sample chapters and tables of contents!

● STAY INFORMED with the latest computer industry news through our online newsletter, press releases, and customized Information SuperLibrary Reports.

● GET FAST ANSWERS to your questions about Hayden books.

● VISIT our online bookstore for the latest information and editions!

● COMMUNICATE with our expert authors through email and conferences.

● DOWNLOAD SOFTWARE from the immence Macmillan Computer Publishing library:
  - Source code, shareware, freeware, and demos.

● DISCOVER HOT SPOTS on other parts of the Internet.

● WIN BOOKS in ongoing contests and giveaways!

TO PLUG INTO HAYDEN:

WORLD WIDE WEB: **http://www.mcp.com/hayden/**

FTP: ftp.mcp.com

REGISTRATION CARD

Photoshop Textures Magic

Hayden
Books

Name _____ Title _____

Company_____Type of business _____

Address _____

City/State/ZIP _____

Have you used these types of books before? ☐ yes ☐ no

If yes, which ones? _____

_____

How many computer books do you purchase each year? ☐ 1–5 ☐ 6 or more

How did you learn about this book? _____

☐ recommended by a friend   ☐ received ad in mail
☐ recommended by store personnel   ☐ read book review
☐ saw in catalog   ☐ saw on bookshelf

Where did you purchase this book? _____

Which applications do you currently use? _____

Which computer magazines do you subscribe to? _____

What trade shows do you attend? _____

Please number the top three factors which most influenced your decision for this book purchase.

☐ cover   ☐ price
☐ approach to content   ☐ author's reputation
☐ logo   ☐ publisher's reputation
☐ layout/design   ☐ other _____

Would you like to be placed on our preferred mailing list? ☐ yes ☐ no email address _____

☐ **I would like to see my name in print!** You may use my name and quote me in future Hayden products and promotions. My daytime phone number is: _____

Comments _____

_____

Hayden Books Attn: Product Marketing ◆ 201 West 103rd Street ◆ Indianapolis, Indiana 46290 USA

Fax to **317-581-3576**   Visit our Web Page **http://www.mcp.com/hayden/**

Fold Here

- -

BUSINESS REPLY MAIL
FIRST-CLASS MAIL PERMIT NO. 9918 INDIANAPOLIS IN

POSTAGE WILL BE PAID BY THE ADDRESSEE

HAYDEN BOOKS
Attn: Product Marketing
201 W 103RD ST
INDIANAPOLIS IN 46290-9058

MACMILLAN COMPUTER PUBLISHING USA

A VIACOM COMPANY

Technical ---- Support:

If you cannot get the CD-ROM/Disk to install properly, or you need assistance with a particular situation in the book, please feel free to check out the Knowledge Base on our Web site at **http://www.superlibrary.com/general/support**. We have answers to our most Frequently Asked Questions listed there. If you do not find your specific question answered, please contact Macmillan Technical Support at **(317) 581-3833**. We can also be reached by email at **support@mcp.com**.